D1481378

Prehistoric Flying Reptiles

Titles in THE DINOSAUR LIBRARY Series

THE DINOSAUR LIBRARY

Prehistoric Flying Reptiles

The Pterosaurs

Thom Holmes and Laurie Holmes

Illustrated by Michael William Skrepnick

Series Advisor:
Dr. Peter Dodson
Professor of Veterinary Anatomy and Paleontology,
University of Pennsylvania
and
co-editor of *The Dinosauria*,
the leading reference used by dinosaur scientists

Enslow Publishers, Inc.

40 Industrial Road   PO Box 38
Box 398   Aldershot
Berkeley Heights, NJ 07922 Hants GU12 6BP
USA   UK

http://www.enslow.com

Copyright © 2003 by Thom Holmes and Laurie Holmes
Illustrations © 2003 by Michael William Skrepnick

All rights reserved.

No part of this book may be reproduced by any means
without the written permission of the publisher.

Library of Congress Cataloging-in-Publication Data

Holmes, Thom.
    Prehistoric flying reptiles : the pterosaurs / Thom Holmes and Laurie Holmes;
    illustrated by Michael William Skrepnick.
        p. cm. — (The dinosaur library)
    Includes bibliographical references and index.
    ISBN 0-7660-2072-X
    1. Pterosauria—Juvenile literature. [1. Pterosaurs. 2. Prehistoric animals.]
    I. Holmes, Laurie. II. Skrepnick, Michael William, ill. III. Title. II. Series: Holmes,
    Thom. Dinosaur library.
    QE862.P7 H65 2003
    567.918—dc21
                                        2002006787

Printed in the United States of America

10 9 8 7 6 5 4 3 2 1

To Our Readers: We have done our best to make sure all Internet Addresses in this book were active and appropriate when we went to press. However, the author and the publisher have no control over and assume no liability for the material available on those Internet sites or on other Web sites they may link to. Any comments or suggestions can be sent by e-mail to comments@enslow.com or to the address on the back cover.

Illustration Credits: Michael William Skrepnick; Illustration on p. 53 after Wellnhofer 1978.

Photo Credits: © Corel Corporation, pp. 8–9, 34, 70; Wayne Grady, p. 6 (Thom Holmes); Shaina Holmes, p. 6 (Laurie Holmes); Thom Holmes, pp. 23, 68, 77, 81; Michael Tropea, p. 7.

Cover Illustration: Michael William Skrepnick

A special thank you goes to Ben Creisler for his help in finalizing the list of genera, pronunciations, and name translations for the pterosaurs included in this book. See the Internet Addresses section for links to Ben's excellent online pronunciation guides for dinosaurs, pterosaurs, marine reptiles, and other prehistoric animals.

Y 567.918 H738p 2003
Holmes, Thom.
Prehistoric flying reptiles
the pterosaurs

CONTENTS

About the Authors

Thom Holmes is a natural history writer specializing in dinosaur science. He has dug for dinosaurs with leading paleontologists in the United States and South America. He has collaborated with Dr. Peter Dodson on several dinosaur-related projects during the past fifteen years.

Laurie Holmes is a science writer and editor, as well as a reading specialist. It has been her privilege to associate with many of the world's leading dinosaur scientists and artists through her work with Thom. Originally a teacher, she maintains that she is still teaching by writing and editing books for young adults.

On a dig in Patagonia, Thom Holmes holds part of the skull bone of what is currently known as the largest meat-eating dinosaur ever.

Thom Holmes

Laurie Holmes

Authors' Note

In writing *The Dinosaur Library*, we enjoyed sharing the knowledge that allows scientists to understand what dinosaurs and pterosaurs were really like. The series covers all the suborders of dinosaurs, from the meat-eating theropods, such as *Tyrannosaurus rex*, to the gigantic plant eaters. It also includes the pterosaurs, flying reptiles that lived during the same time as the dinosaurs. We hope you enjoy learning about these fascinating creatures that ruled the earth for 160 million years.

ABOUT THE ILLUSTRATOR

Michael William Skrepnick is an established paleo artist with a lifelong interest in dinosaurs. He has worked on newly described dinosaurs with a number of the world's leading paleontologists. His original artworks are found in a number of art collections and reproduced as museum murals, and in popular books, magazines, scientific journals, and television documentaries.  Michael lives and works in Alberta, Canada, close to some of the richest Upper Cretaceous dinosaur fossil localities in the world.

✦ ✦ ✦

Paleo art is a field devoted to the reconstruction and life restoration of long extinct animals and their environments. Since we cannot observe dinosaurs (other than living birds) in nature, we may never truly know their habits, lifestyles, or the color of their skin. In addition, the fossil record provides only a fraction of the remains of a wide diversity of life on earth.

Many fairly complete skeletons of dinosaurs have been unearthed in recent history. Others are represented by as little as a fragment of a single fractured bone, an isolated tooth, or a footprint impressed in once-wet mud. It is still possible to create a reliable portrait of unique, previously unknown creatures, but the accuracy of the art depends on the following:

- The quality and amount of actual skeletal material of the specimen preserved
- Discussion and collaboration with a paleontologist familiar with the fossil material and locality from which it was excavated
- Observation and comparisons to the closest related living forms
- The technical abilities, skill, and disciplined vision of the artist

The resulting artwork can draw the viewer back in time into exotic worlds of the ancient.

THE CLIFF PERCH

*H*igh on a cliff overlooking the Tethys Sea, a female Pterodactylus *sat on her brood of eggs. There were three eggs in all, small and oval. Her nest was one of many positioned along the wide cliff shelf. There were dozens of other pterosaurs watching over their nests as well.*

The mother had an itch on her belly and tried to scratch the brown furry spot with her beak. Even with her long twisty neck, the itch was just a little out of reach. She gently rustled her wings against her lower torso to make the itch go away.

The eggs in the nests needed to stay warm. The mother accomplished this for part of the day by gently sitting on top of them. Her warm body safeguarded the tiny embryos maturing inside the eggs.

The morning was cool until the sun rose over the top of the cliff to shine directly on the nesting area. Most of the nests still had eggs that were not hatched. The mother waited patiently for the afternoon sun to bathe her nest in warmth. That was her cue to go fishing. The sun would keep the nest warm while she went for food.

The mother ambled over to the edge of the cliff, walking awkwardly on four legs. With a slight waddle to her step, she approached the breezy, wide-open space that separated her from the ocean far below. Another female approached the edge with her. This one had a streak of gray hair running down her neck. As each of them felt ready to go, she leaned into the strong crosswind that whipped past the cliff. Unfolding their wings, they swooped out together and began to flap. After clearing the jagged cliff edge, they soared on the wind out toward the open ocean.

The mother peered down with her keen eyes. The sea was jumping with fish. She could see the white splashes of a large school of small fish as they frequently leaped out of the water. That was her signal to descend. Gray Neck took the cue as well, and together they swooped down, cutting through the wind.

Patience was required for fishing. Jabbing blindly at the water did not usually work, although some of the older pterosaurs, their eyes not as sharp as they once were, often resorted to this tactic. But the two mothers were young and strong.

They came at the school of fish from the side, against the direction in which the fish were swimming. This gave them the best chance of snatching up a prey. The teeth of Pterodactylus *were small, requiring the reptiles to attack with precise snatches of the mouth.*

Low, low, low they swept. First the mother and then Gray

Neck came up with a small fish. They ate them quickly as they flapped their wings to gain altitude for another strike. By the time they had scaled the wind again, they had finished their snacks. It was time for more.

Again they swept down at an angle to the direction of the school of fish. Gray Neck had descended first. The other mother could see Gray Neck closing in on the school of fish. Gray Neck opened her mouth slightly to prepare for her strike.

Without warning, a large fish about three times the size of Gray Neck surged from the water and clamped down on her wings with its long gaping jaws. Gray Neck shrieked in surprise but was dragged underwater by the hungry fish. The other mother watched Gray Neck's wings disappear in a white splash.

The mother was distracted by what she had seen. Another large fish with gaping jaws was leaping out of the water at her. She noticed the fish just in time. She shifted her wings and flapped madly to escape the jaws of the giant fish. As she desperately rose above the leaping predator, she could hear a gasping sound from its mouth as it passed by, jaws wide open, white bristling teeth snapping as it passed. Its tail brushed against the mother's wing as the fish fell back into the water. But she had escaped Gray Neck's fate.

The mother flew up to a safe height and circled the area, looking for other fish. She stayed away from large schools, at least for the rest of the day. Somehow, she had learned that lesson. After a few more passes, she had filled her throat pouch with several small fish and returned to her nest to eat at her leisure.

Gray Neck's nest remained unattended. Without their mother

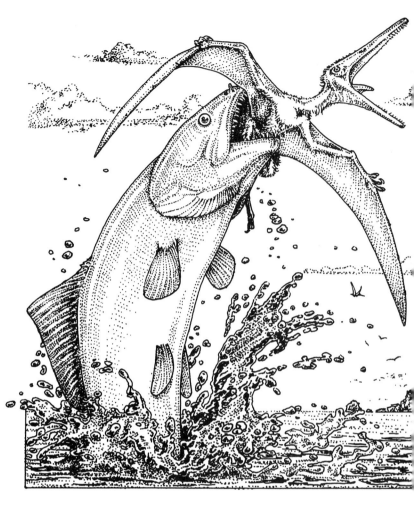

to warm them at night, the embryos inside Gray Neck's eggs would soon die.

Long after the other mother's eggs had hatched, Gray Neck's remained in their nest, weathering away.

Authors' Note—The preceding story is fiction but is based on scientific evidence and ideas suggested by paleontologists. You will find explanations to support these ideas in the chapters that follow.

- Kinds of flying reptiles: Chapter 2 (The Many Families of Flying Reptiles)

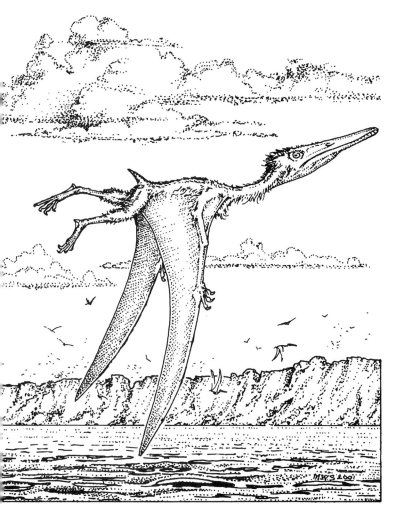

- Geographic locations: Chapter 2 (Where Did Flying Reptiles Live?)

- Furry body covering: Chapter 3 (Anatomy of the Flying Reptiles)

- Walking and flying: Chapters 3 (Anatomy of the Flying Reptiles) and 4 (Lifestyle and Physiology of the Flying Reptiles)

- Pterosaur eggs and babies: Chapter 5 (Eggs and Babies)

- Hunting and eating habits: Chapter 6 (Feeding Habits and Adaptations)

CHAPTER 1

REPTILES OF THE SKY

What were the pterosaurs? These close relatives of dinosaurs were the first vertebrates—backboned animals—to fly. They lived during the span of the age of dinosaurs, and their remains are often found in the same fossil deposits as their giant, earthbound neighbors. Like the dinosaurs, they were a special kind of reptile that no longer exists today.

Pterosaurs, the flying reptiles, were *not* dinosaurs. They were also not related to birds. Certain small meat-eating dinosaurs were actually more closely related to birds than the pterosaurs. The fact that both pterosaurs and birds had the ability to fly is a good example of *convergent evolution*. Convergent evolution happens when different kinds of animals, although otherwise unrelated, adapt to their environment by evolving similar body features.

Although pterosaurs were not dinosaurs, they are sometimes called "flying dinosaurs" by mistake. They were probably related to a common ancestor of the dinosaurs, but pterosaurs had several features that made them different. A proper definition of the pterosaurs takes into account the following:

Pterosaurs lived only during the Mesozoic Era. The age of pterosaurs was approximately the same as the age of dinosaurs. It spanned from the Late Triassic Period about 225 million years ago to the end of the Late Cretaceous Period, some 65 million years ago. This means that all pterosaurs are *extinct.*

Flying reptiles were not dinosaurs. They were special reptiles that lived millions of years ago. Pteranodon was a giant, toothless pterosaur.

Pterosaurs were a special kind of reptile. Pterosaurs had some characteristics common to all reptiles. Most importantly, their skulls were similar to those of other reptiles. Pterosaurs also had a backbone, and they probably laid eggs like all known reptiles.

Pterosaurs could fly. Pterosaurs were the first vertebrates that could fly.

Pterosaurs had special skeletal features. Pterosaurs came in a wide range of sizes, from those with a 1-foot (0.3-meter) wingspan to giants that could dwarf the largest of today's birds. Even though they came in many sizes, however, all pterosaurs had common traits, such as skeletons suited for powered flight and lightweight, hollow bones. These skeletal features are listed in Chapter 3.

Understanding Pterosaurs

Our knowledge of pterosaurs begins with their fossilized skeletons. Fortunately, many pterosaurs have been discovered with their bones in the proper places, giving us an accurate picture of what they looked like. Because pterosaurs were vertebrates, their skeletons are similar in some ways to other animals with which we are more familiar. A basic knowledge of vertebrate skeletons helps guide the paleontologist in putting the pieces of a fossil skeleton together accurately.

The study of fossil organisms is called *paleontology*. *Paleo* means "ancient." Paleontologists use fossil traces of ancient organisms as a window onto life in the distant past, before the evolution of modern man.

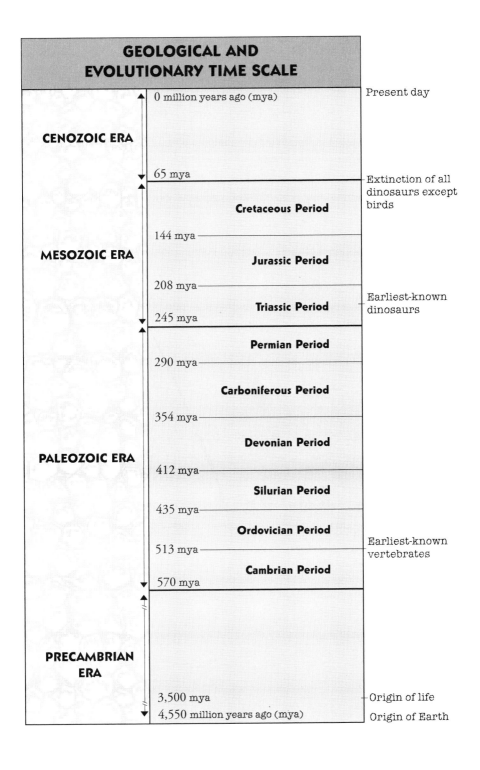

GEOLOGICAL AND EVOLUTIONARY TIME SCALE

0 million years ago (mya) — Present day

CENOZOIC ERA

65 mya — Extinction of all dinosaurs except birds

MESOZOIC ERA

Cretaceous Period

144 mya

Jurassic Period

208 mya

Triassic Period — Earliest-known dinosaurs

245 mya

PALEOZOIC ERA

Permian Period

290 mya

Carboniferous Period

354 mya

Devonian Period

412 mya

Silurian Period

435 mya

Ordovician Period

513 mya — Earliest-known vertebrates

Cambrian Period

570 mya

PRECAMBRIAN ERA

3,500 mya — Origin of life

4,550 million years ago (mya) — Origin of Earth

One disadvantage of studying pterosaurs is that their fossil remains are scarce when compared to those of dinosaurs. One reason for the scarcity of pterosaur fossils is that their light-weight bones were less likely to survive the fossilization process. This has much to do with the place where the animal died. If a pterosaur's body fell into shallow water or a shoreline environment, it was more likely to be preserved than one that fell inland. A watery environment would have gently buried the skeleton with mud and silt, protecting it and making fossilization possible. A pterosaur that died on land would have been exposed to harsher conditions that would have destroyed most if its remains before they could be buried.

There are only a little more than 55 well-understood kinds, or genera, of pterosaurs, compared to over 350 genera of dinosaurs. This does not mean that there were not more varieties of pterosaurs. Because they were usually preserved only in the watery sediment found near large bodies of water, most evidence is only for pterosaurs that lived by the shore.

While no human being has ever seen a pterosaur in the flesh, paleontologists can uncover many secrets by studying the fossil clues. A paleontologist must have a firm grasp of scientific methods and fact. He or she must also have a good imagination and a knack for solving mysteries. Fossils provide evidence for the construction of pterosaurs. The paleontologist examines these facts and tries to understand how they affected the pterosaur's way of life.

The Pterosaurs

Pterosaurs were discovered many years before *dinosaurs* became a household word. The first scientific description of a pterosaur fossil is from 1784 for a specimen discovered in Germany. The specimen was discovered in Bavaria in the Solnhofen region, famous for its limestone quarries. This is the same general area in which *Archaeopteryx* ("ancient feather"), the first bird, was discovered more than seventy-five years later, in 1861. This was also forty years before the first dinosaur would be described by William Buckland in England in 1824.

Archaeopteryx was the first known bird. The first flying reptile was discovered even earlier than this first bird, in the same general area in Germany.

The pterosaur in question was described by Italian naturalist Cosimo Alessandro Collini. It had a long, toothed snout and a wingspan of about 3 feet (1 meter). Collini did not know what to make of it, because nothing like it had ever been discovered before. All he knew for sure was that it was unlike any bird, mammal, reptile, or other vertebrate that had ever lived.

Several other scientists took a stab at describing the pterosaur. One thought it was a waterbird, another thought it was a bat. It wasn't until the famous French scientist Georges Cuvier took a careful look at the fossil in 1812 that its true nature was understood. Cuvier explained that the pterosaur was a newly discovered form of extinct reptile. He named it *Pterodactylus* ("wing finger") after the long fourth finger that made up the length of the wing. It had a short tail.

The Solnhofen region in Bavaria is famous for the exquisitely preserved fossils of many small kinds of pterosaurs, dinosaurs, reptiles, amphibians, plants, fish, marine invertebrates,

Pterodactylus

and insects. It had been a tropical lagoon about 145 million years ago in the Late Jurassic Period. The creatures that died and fell into the water were evidently buried quickly by mud, preserving the finest details of their skeletal structures. In the case of *Archaeopteryx*, the preservation was so fine that the impressions of long-vanished feathers could still be seen in the rock.

The wonderfully preserved fossils from the limestone quarries of Solnhofen continued to reveal new specimens of pterosaurs. By 1847, with the discovery of the first known pterosaur with a long tail, *Rhamphorhynchus* ("beak snout"), it had become clear that two basic forms of pterosaur existed. Some had short tails and some had long tails. The short-tailed variety is part of a group called Pterodactyloidea. Pterosaurs with long tails are part of a group called Rhamphorhynchoidea. Both groups are named after the first important specimens discovered in their categories.

The evolution of the two forms of pterosaurs occurred during the same time as the evolution of the dinosaurs.

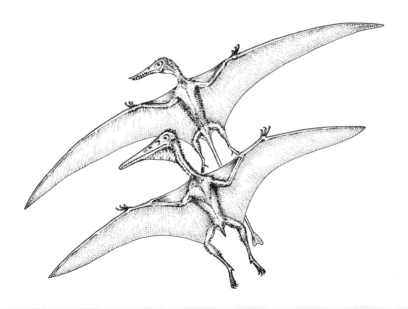

Rhamphorhynchus (top) was a long-tailed pterosaur; Pterodactylus was a short-tailed pterosaur.

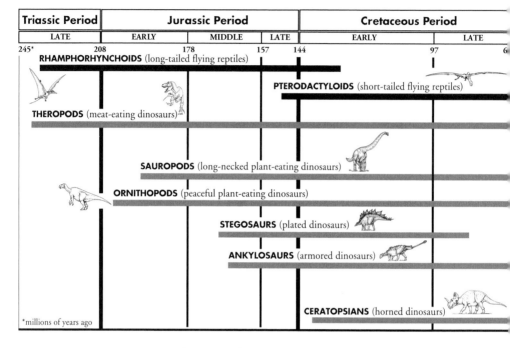

Triassic Period		Jurassic Period			Cretaceous Period	
LATE	EARLY	MIDDLE		LATE	EARLY	LATE

245*   208   178   157   144   97   6

RHAMPHORHYNCHOIDS (long-tailed flying reptiles)

PTERODACTYLOIDS (short-tailed flying reptiles)

THEROPODS (meat-eating dinosaurs)

SAUROPODS (long-necked plant-eating dinosaurs)

ORNITHOPODS (peaceful plant-eating dinosaurs)

STEGOSAURS (plated dinosaurs)

ANKYLOSAURS (armored dinosaurs)

CERATOPSIANS (horned dinosaurs)

*millions of years ago

Pterosaurs existed in one form or another throughout nearly the entire age of dinosaurs—from the Late Triassic to the end of the Late Cretaceous Periods.

In coexisting with their dinosaur cousins for so many millions of years, some pterosaurs evolved that did not compete directly with the dinosaurs for either food or living space. They seemed to have filled a role in the environment as fish eaters and possible carrion eaters. They lived on cliffs and other out-of-the-way places where dinosaurs did not tread. This is not to say that the dinosaurs and pterosaurs did not ultimately compete for survival. The extinction of the smaller pterosaurs may have been affected by a new kind of dinosaur that rose during the age of dinosaurs: the smaller, quicker, and probably smarter birds.

CHAPTER 2

THE MANY FAMILIES OF FLYING REPTILES

Pterosaurs and their dinosaur cousins fall within the class of vertebrates known as Reptilia, or reptiles. Reptiles are egg-laying backboned animals with scaly skin. The different kinds of reptiles, living and extinct, are grouped by certain features of their skeletons. Most important is the design of the reptilian skull. Pterosaurs fall within the subclass Diapsida, which includes reptiles whose skulls have a pair of openings behind each eye. Diapsida is divided into two groups: the lepidosaurs and the archosaurs. Lepidosaurs consist of the kinds of lizards and snakes that live today. Archosaurs consist of thecodonts (a group of reptiles from the Triassic Period), crocodiles (living and extinct), pterosaurs (extinct flying reptiles), and dinosaurs (extinct except for birds).

All pterosaurs are probably descendants of a single common archosaurian ancestor not yet identified.[1] They differed from dinosaurs in that they developed hip, breast, shoulder, and limb bones optimized for flying. In contrast, even the earliest dinosaurs had evolved hip and limb bones that made them sturdy, capable walkers, a factor that allowed them eventually to evolve to enormous sizes. This suggests pterosaur ancestors branched off from the reptilian family tree before the appearance of the first dinosaurs.

The pterosaurs and other diapsid reptiles were some of the most successful land vertebrates of all time. Pterosaurs first appeared about 220 million years ago and began to spread rapidly by the end of the Triassic Period. Figure 1 summarizes the evolution of vertebrates leading to the pterosaurs.

Pterosaur Beginnings and Evolution

The earliest archosaurs were meat eaters. Some evolved with four sprawling legs; others gradually began to walk or sprint for short distances on their two hind legs. By the Late Triassic Period, about 225 million years ago, some two-legged, meat-eating creatures had evolved specialized hips and legs to help them stand erect. This supported the full weight of their bodies while they walked on two feet. They ranged in size from about 6 inches (15 centimeters) to 13 feet (4 meters). It is likely that the pterosaurs, like their dinosaur cousins, evolved from these early reptiles.

But how did a land creature become a flying one? Unfortunately, the fossil record has so far been silent on this

Evolutionary Steps
Leading to Pterosaurs

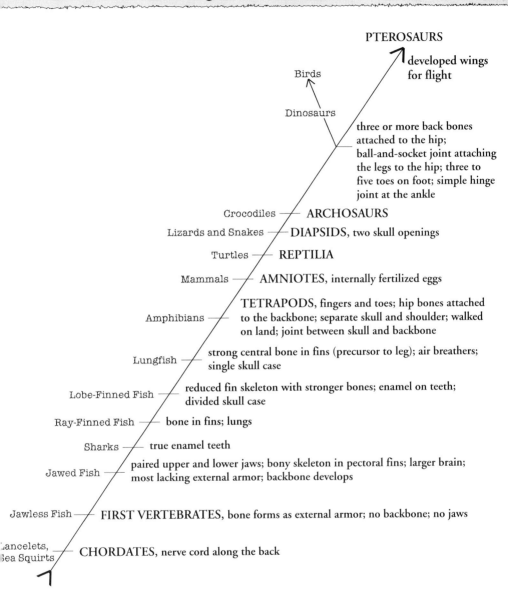

PTEROSAURS

developed wings
for flight

Birds

Dinosaurs

three or more back bones
attached to the hip;
ball-and-socket joint attaching
the legs to the hip; three to
five toes on foot; simple hinge
joint at the ankle

Crocodiles — ARCHOSAURS

Lizards and Snakes — DIAPSIDS, two skull openings

Turtles — REPTILIA

Mammals — AMNIOTES, internally fertilized eggs

TETRAPODS, fingers and toes; hip bones attached
Amphibians — to the backbone; separate skull and shoulder; walked
on land; joint between skull and backbone

Lungfish — strong central bone in fins (precursor to leg); air breathers;
single skull case

Lobe-Finned Fish — reduced fin skeleton with stronger bones; enamel on teeth;
divided skull case

Ray-Finned Fish — bone in fins; lungs

Sharks — true enamel teeth

Jawed Fish — paired upper and lower jaws; bony skeleton in pectoral fins; larger brain;
most lacking external armor; backbone develops

Jawless Fish — FIRST VERTEBRATES, bone forms as external armor; no backbone; no jaws

Lancelets,
Sea Squirts — CHORDATES, nerve cord along the back

Figure 1. This diagram shows how vertebrate animals evolved to yield
pterosaurs. The steps along the way include evolutionary changes that are
directly related to the traits of pterosaurs. The time span from the appearance
of the first chordates (animals with primitive backbones) to the last pterosaur
is about 460 million years.

matter. While there are several early archosaurs that appear to be related to the evolution of the pterosaurs and dinosaurs, scientists have not yet found a clearly identifiable ancestor of the pterosaurs. What clues would they be looking for? Such a creature would probably have started to evolve longer front legs than hind legs as a step toward the development of wings. An early stage of this evolution may have been a tree-climbing archosaur that developed a wing membrane for gliding. This may have led to the evolution of wings for powered flight in pterosaurs. (Pterosaurs were not gliders. They could flap their wings for powered flight.) The same process may have taken place again many of millions of years later in the evolution of birds.

The earliest form of pterosaurs had appeared by the Late Triassic Period. They were the long-tailed rhamphorhynchoids. By the Late Jurassic Period, the short-tailed pterodactyloids had evolved. The pterodactyloids developed into larger and larger flying reptiles. The largest of these have been discovered inland, far from the coastal shores where earlier pterosaurs thrived. The large pterosaurs may have become carrion eaters—giant pterosaurian vultures. As the pterodactyloids evolved during the early part of the Cretaceous Period, the smaller rhamphorhynchoids became extinct. They may have been competing with birds, which were beginning to spread widely at the same time.

The fossil record is very spotty for pterosaurs, making it difficult for scientists to draw clear connections in the family tree of these creatures. An understanding of the pterosaur family tree will improve as more fossils are discovered to fill in the gaps. At this time, however, scientists describe the best-known families and kinds of pterosaurs and list them according to whether they have long tails or short tails.

Where Did Flying Reptiles Live?

When the pterosaurs first appeared during the Late Triassic Period, the continents that we know today were still joined together as one supercontinent known as Pangaea. By the end of the Mesozoic Era, when the last of the pterosaurs perished, the continents had broken apart to form the major landmasses known today as North and South America, Africa, Europe, Asia, Australia, and Antarctica. During the 180 million years that it took for the earth to make this physical transformation, the habitat of the pterosaurs, including the shorelines of oceans, changed dramatically.

When the continents were one landmass, it was possible for pterosaurs to spread to most corners of the earth. The remains of pterosaurs have been discovered on every continent except Antarctica. Pterosaurs spread rapidly around the globe while the continents were still connected. By the middle and later parts of the Cretaceous Period, when the largest of the winged reptiles appeared, the Northern and Southern Hemispheres had split apart. Although pterosaurs could fly, the separation of these landmasses made their migration from the Northern Hemisphere to the Southern Hemisphere less likely. Today's arrangement of the continents was substantially formed during the end of the Cretaceous Period, the end of the era of pterosaurs and dinosaurs.

Pterosaur
Locations
the

Fossil
Around
World

RHAMPHORHYNCHOIDEA (LONG-TAILED PTEROSAURS)

Eudimorphodontidae ("true two-form tooth")

Some of the earliest known pterosaurs, these small flyers had a wingspan of about 3.3 feet (1 meter). They had teeth of various sizes, with one, three, or five cusps. They probably ate insects and fish. Found in Italy.

Time: Late Triassic.

Eudimorphodon

Dimorphodontidae ("two-form tooth")

Peteinosaurus

These primitive long-tailed pterosaurs had a short wingspan, strong claws for grasping and climbing, and a stiffened tail. The head was tall and rounded, like a puffin's. It had widely spaced, pointed teeth of various sizes for eating fish. Found in Italy and the United Kingdom.

Time: Late Triassic to Early Jurassic.

Dimorphodon

Rhamphorhynchoidae ("beak snout")

This family had long, narrow jaws filled with sharp, widely spaced teeth that pointed outward, probably to spear fish as it skimmed over the water. Their tails had a flat, vertical rudder. Found in Germany, England, Italy, Portugal, Central Asia, and Tanzania.

Angustinaripterus, Campylognathoides, Preondactylus, Rhamphorhynchus, Scaphognathus, Sordes

Time: Late Triassic to Middle Jurassic.

Dorygnathus

Anurognathidae ("tailless jaw")

Even though this poorly known family had a short tail, paleontologists believe it was most closely related to the rhamphorhynchoids. These pterosaurs had peglike teeth, probably for eating insects. They were small, with a wingspan of only 20 inches (51 centimeters), and had a rounded head. Found in Germany and Central Asia.

Anurognathus, Batrachognathus

Time: Late Jurassic.

Other Rhamphorhynchoidea

Not enough is known yet about these reptiles to place them into families.

Comodactylus, Herbstosaurus, Nesodactylus, Rhamphinion

PTERODACTYLOIDEA (SHORT-TAILED PTEROSAURS)

Pterodactylidae ("wing finger")

Many species of Pterodactylus have been found. They had long jaws with forward-pointing teeth suited for eating fish or insects. They were small, with a wingspan of about 15 inches (39 centimeters). They had long necks and were agile flyers. Found in Germany, France, England, and Tanzania.

Time: Late Jurassic.

Pterodactylus

Gallodactylidae ("Gallic finger")

This pterosaur was distinguished by a short bony crest running along the back of the skull and closely spaced, forward-pointing teeth that were set in the front of the jaws. It had a wingspan of 4.4 feet (1.4 meters). Found in Germany and France.

Time: Late Jurassic.

Gallodactylus

Germanodactylidae ("German finger")

Similar to Pterodactylus, this pterosaur had a long, low crest on top of its head, but it was larger, with a wingspan of 3.5 feet (about 1 meter). Its teeth were forward pointing for grasping fish. Found in Germany and England.

Time: Late Jurassic.

Germanodactylus

Ctenochasmatidae ("comb jaws")

Ranging in wingspan from about 4 to 8 feet (1.2 to 2.4 meters), each member of this family had long jaws with a basket of closely packed teeth at the front of its upper and lower jaws. The teeth could filter out small aquatic animals from the water. Found in Germany, France, and China.

Time: Late Jurassic.

*Ctenochasma,
Gnathosaurus,
Huanhepterus*

Pterodaustridae ("southern wing")

This moderate-sized pterosaur had a wingspan of 4.3 feet (1.3 meters) and a highly specialized lower jaw for filter feeding. Hundreds of upward-pointing teeth in the lower jaw formed a long basket for filtering out small creatures from the water. Found in Argentina and Chile.

Time: Early Cretaceous.

Pterodaustro

PTERODACTYLOIDEA (SHORT-TAILED PTEROSAURS), con't.

Dsungaripteridae ("Junggar Basin wing")

With wingspans measuring from about 5 to 10 feet (1.5 to 3 meters), members of this family had a short crest and a long, pointed jaw that curved upward. The curved jaw and sturdy teeth could be used like a nutcracker to crack open hard-shelled creatures. Found in China, Central Asia, Tanzania, Brazil, and Argentina.

Time: Late Jurassic to Early Cretaceous.

Noripterus, Phobetor, Puntanipterus

Dsungaripterus

Ornithocheiridae ("bird hand")

A moderate-sized pterosaur with a wingspan of up to 8.2 feet (2.5 meters), it had a long jaw with short teeth and was one of the most widespread pterosaurs in the world. Found in England, Austria, Germany, France, Australia, Argentina, Brazil, New Zealand, and Zaire.

Time: Early to Late Cretaceous.

Araripesaurus, Brasileodactylus, Santanadactylus

Ornithocheirus

Anhangueridae ("old devil")

This moderately large pterosaur had a wide wingspan of 13 feet (4 meters). Its long, toothed jaw had round crests running the length of the top of the upper jaw and the bottom of the lower jaw. These crests may have acted like a rudder to stabilize the animal's flight while it plowed its head through the water to catch fish. Found in Brazil.

Time: Early Cretaceous.

Anhanguera

Criorhynchidae ("ram snout")

Large, toothed pterosaurs with wingspans measuring from 16.4 to 20 feet (5 to 6 meters). They had a rounded crest on the top and bottom front parts of their jaws, which may have acted like a rudder to steady them as they dipped their nose in the water for fish. Found in England and Brazil.

Time: Early to Late Cretaceous.

Criorhynchus

Tropeognathus

Tapejaridae ("ancient being")

Toothless pterosaurs with a long, bony crest running along the top of the nose. The ends of the jaws pointed downward, like those of some birds. These are only known from skull fragments. Found in Brazil.

Time: Early Cretaceous.

Tapejara, Tupuxuara

PTEROSAUR FAMILIES	SOME MEMBERS
Cearadactylidae ("Ceará [Brazil] finger") his moderately large pterosaur is known only from its skull. he front teeth are much longer than its back teeth, forming a t of "claws" at the front of its mouth with which it could grab sh. Found in Brazil. me: Early Cretaceous.	*Cearadactylus*
Ornithodesmidae ("bird ribbon") family of large pterosaurs with a wingspan of up to 16.4 feet meters). The front of its beak was rounded like that of a duck. s short, widely spaced teeth were set in the front half of the pper and lower jaws and would mesh when the jaws were osed. Its eyes were small for pterosaurs of this size. The first six rtebrae of its back were fused and served as a solid anchor to hich limb muscles were attached. Found in England. me: Early Cretaceous.	*Ornithodesmus*
Pteranodontidae ("toothless flyer") his giant, toothless pterosaur had a wingspan ranging from 23 30 feet (7 to 9 meters). It has been found with a variety of rge, angular crests on the back of its head. Found in Kansas, Iontana, Oregon, Georgia, Delaware, Alberta, England, entral Asia, Peru, Australia, and Japan. me: Early to Late Cretaceous.	*Ornithostoma* *Pteranodon*
Nyctosauridae ("night reptile") family of moderately sized pterosaurs with a wingspan of 9.5 et (2.8 meters). It was toothless and had a short crest on the ack of its head. Found in Kansas and Brazil. me: Late Cretaceous.	*Nyctosaurus*
Azhdarchidae ("dragon") his group represents the giants of the pterosaurs, including uetzalcoatlus, which had a wingspan of 36 to 39 feet (11 to 12 eters). These toothless giants appear to have lived inland, here they fed either from streams or from carrion. Found in gland, Jordan, Central Asia, Texas, and Alberta. me: Early to Late Cretaceous.	*Arambourgiania,* *Azhdarcho,* *Doratorhynchus,* *Quetzalcoatlus*
Other Pterodactyloidea t enough is known about these reptiles to place them into families.	*Araripedactylus,* *Dermodactylus,* *Mesadactylus*

CHAPTER 3

ANATOMY OF THE FLYING REPTILES

Pterosaurs shared many skeletal features with other vertebrates, living and extinct. Even though scientists only rarely see the fossil evidence of soft tissue or organs of the fossil vertebrates—such as the lungs, heart, or gut—they can assume that these parts were similar to those of today's vertebrates. By fitting what they know about today's vertebrates into the patchy evidence they have of fossilized vertebrates, scientists can understand what a living pterosaur was really like.

The most distinctive difference between pterosaurs and all other reptiles was their ability to fly. How did their land-dwelling ancestors develop the ability to soar through the air on powerful wings? Powered flight has evolved in several kinds of vertebrates, but the pterosaurs were the first back-boned animals with this amazing ability.

The Evolution of Flight

Animal flight can be achieved in three ways: gliding, soaring, and powered flight.[1] Gliding uses large airfoils—wings—to suspend an animal in the air for a slow descent. Soaring uses wings designed to allow a creature to rise and fall on air currents. Wings designed for powered flight require vigorous flapping to stay aloft but may also make some gliding and soaring possible. Some birds, such as gulls and albatrosses, use powered flight for taking off, but soar to stay aloft for long periods.

Powered flight is not unique to modern birds. Insects, bats, and pterosaurs all fly (or flew) under their own power. Among animals with backbones, powered flight has evolved three separate times—first in pterosaurs, then in birds, and finally in bats—each independent of the others. This is called *convergent evolution* and means that different kinds of animals, although otherwise unrelated, adapted to their environment by evolving similar anatomical features.

There are three anatomical requirements for powered flight:

Lightweight body. Pterosaurs, birds, and bats have hollow bones and sometimes fewer bones in the back, which makes them lighter than other animals of similar size.

Airfoil to produce lift. The wing is an airfoil. When combined with forward motion, it produces lift, the force that allows a body to become airborne.

Energy to take off. Most modern birds are strong enough to become airborne from a standing start. Just how the

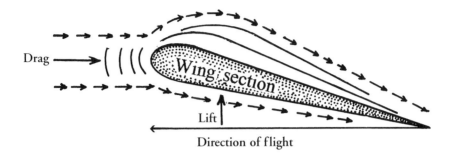

Drag →

Wing section

Lift ↑

Direction of flight

This wing is viewed in cross section. Notice that the curved upper surface of a wing is longer than its flat lower surface. Air moving over the top of the surface must travel farther and faster than the air moving underneath. The difference pulls the wing upward.

pterosaurs took flight depended on their size. The smaller pterosaurs, such as *Rhamphorhynchus*, *Scaphognathus* ("boat jaw"), and *Pterodactylus*, probably took off from the ground, like birds, by flapping their wings. The larger pterosaurs, including *Pteranodon* ("toothless flyer") and *Quetzalcoatlus* ("plumed serpent"), must have been too heavy to take off without assistance from a strong head wind, unless they jumped from a high spot.[2]

Taking Wing for the First Time

There is little debate about the origin of flight in pterosaurs. Being the first known vertebrates with truly powered flight, they most likely evolved from an earlier form of flightless reptile. It is generally accepted that pterosaurs arose from a line of small reptiles that developed primitive wings in the form of skin folds. These skin folds allowed them to glide down from trees. As they became more skilled at gliding, turning their bodies and wings to steer themselves and control their fall, they began to build the physical adaptations that evolved into powered flight. Over time, these small, active creatures developed increasingly powerful wings, along with stronger skeletal structures and muscles to flap them.

The Pterosaur Body

Pterosaurs ranged in size from small, crow-sized creatures with a wingspan of 1 foot (0.3 meters) to giants of the sky with wingspans of up to 39 feet (12 meters), the size of a small airplane. During their time, pterosaurs were the dominant animals of the coastal areas of the world, skimming the oceans for a bounty of fish and other small sea creatures. They may have lived in great nesting colonies, forming a unique place for themselves in a world otherwise ruled by dinosaurs.

As mentioned earlier, the pterosaurs have been divided into two superfamilies based on their physical characteristics. The Rhamphorhynchoidea usually had long tails, although there are exceptions, and were the earliest kinds of pterosaurs to evolve. Most of them lived during the Late Triassic and Jurassic Periods. There is now evidence that some lived during the Early Cretaceous Period as well. The Pterodactyloidea evolved later and were mostly larger than the rhamphorhynchoids. They had short tails and included the largest flying creatures ever to inhabit the earth. Most of the pterodactyloids lived during the Cretaceous Period.

Anatomical features that were common to all pterosaurs include the following:

- Small body, large head, and long limbs.

- Lightweight skull with many openings and very large eyes. The skull was generally long, narrow, and short.

- Hollow bones to reduce body weight, making flight easier. One calculation estimates that a pterosaur with a wingspan of 23 feet (7 meters) had a body weight of only about 37 pounds (17 kilograms).[3]

- Powered wings and specialized bones in the shoulders and breast for the attachment of flight muscles and the reinforcement of wing flapping. The forelimbs that made up the wing had four fingers each. The wings were shaped by the fourth finger of each hand, which was extremely long compared to the other three clawed fingers. Unlike birds and bats, pterosaurs had only one finger of the hand that was lengthened in this way.[4]

- The three fingers of the forelimbs that were not attached to the wing had curved claws for grasping prey or holding tight to a vertical perch, such as a cliff wall.

- A strong neck with seven, eight, or nine vertebrae. Vertebrae of the back (torso) numbered between eleven and sixteen. In later pterosaurs, several of the bones of the upper back were fused together to strengthen the shoulders for flight. Long-tailed pterosaurs had up to forty vertebrae in the tail.

- Large and specially-shaped breastbone to anchor flight muscles. The breastbone of pterosaurs was large but not as pronounced as the breastbone seen later in birds.

- Lightweight and weak hind limbs with five clawed toes on each foot. The leg bones were short when compared to the enormous length of the wings formed by the forelimbs, but proportionately about the same size as those of a two-legged dinosaur when compared to the body size.[5] However, the head, or top, of the thighbone (femur) pointed upward in a most undinosaur-like way, which affected the pterosaurs' posture.

- Long, narrow toes on the hind limbs and an ankle that could bend enough so that the pterosaur could walk on the soles of its feet rather than on its toes like dinosaurs and birds.

- Teeth, when present, had individual sockets. The number, size, and arrangement of teeth varied widely among pterosaurs, but they were often pointed forward to aid in snatching fish. The teeth of the upper

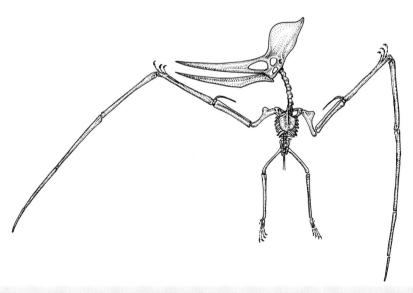

Pteranodon skeleton

and lower jaws often interlocked when the mouth was closed, creating a firm grip on whatever the pterosaur was biting.

- Leathery or hairy body covering. The wing membrane consisted of leathery skin.

The anatomical differences between the Pterodactyloidea and the Rhamphorhynchoidea go beyond the length of the tail. Some of these differences are not obvious to the casual observer. But to the paleontologist, these special differences are clues to the evolution and variety of pterosaurs that thrived for many millions of years. The features that make the two large groups of pterosaurs different from one another are listed in the table on page 41.

Pterosaur Skin

Pterosaur skin, like other soft body parts of these animals, was almost never fossilized. The skin of pterosaurs easily decomposed and disappeared long before fossilization could take place. Although there is some evidence about pterosaur skin, it is extremely rare. Some of the best examples of fossilized skin patterns come from the smooth limestone deposits of Solnhofen in Germany.

A fossilized skin impression is *not* the pterosaur skin itself, but the pattern of the skin that was left behind in the mud or sand where the creature died. Skin impressions are called trace fossils. They represent a trace of the pterosaur that made them, rather than being the fossilized parts of the animal itself.

Unlike dinosaurs, which had reptilelike skin composed of nonoverlapping scales, pterosaurs had leathery skin. From the

Rhamphorhynchoidea (Long-Tailed Pterosaurs)	Pterodactyloidea (Short-Tailed Pterosaurs)
Long tail with elongated vertebrae.	Short tail.
Jaws with teeth. The teeth were often longer in the front of the jaws and pointed forward and outward, ideal for snatching fish from the water.	Some had jaws with many teeth, others had only a few teeth, and some had no teeth at all. The teeth were conical and often pointed forward. Pterodactyloid teeth were generally shorter than those of rhamphorhynchoids, although a few varieties had highly specialized masses of teeth used for filtering food out of the water like a fine fishnet.
A full set of neck ribs.	Only two neck ribs.
No fused back bones in the upper spine.	Several fused back bones in the upper spine, forming a bony structure called a notarium. Although found in small and large pterosaurs alike, this reinforced backbone may have enabled the evolution of large-sized pterosaurs by providing a sturdier back.
Short wrist bones.	Long wrist bones.
The wing finger had a deep groove for the attachment of the wing membrane.	The wing finger does not have a deep groove for the attachment of the wing membrane.
Long fifth toe on foot.	Short fifth toe on foot.

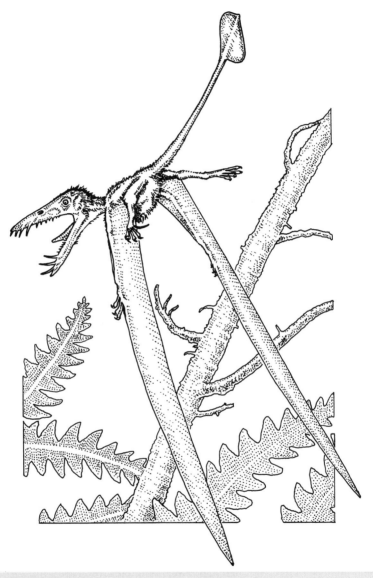

Rhamphorhynchoids, such as this Dorygnathus, were the first vertebrates to master powered flight. They were relatively small in size, often no bigger than a sparrow. They usually had long tails with a rudderlike tail flap to stabilize their flight.

earliest discoveries of pterosaurs, scientists wondered if this skin may have been covered with an insulating layer of fur or feathers. Such a coating would have helped the creatures retain body heat, an important factor for an active flyer. In 1970, a fossil of a small pterosaur provided possible evidence that these creatures had been covered with hair. The specimen in question is the remarkable *Sordes* ("hairy devil"), a small rhamphorhynchoid from Central Asia. What may be the evidence of hair appears as finely patterned impressions in the fossil. *Sordes* seemed to have had furry wings with a dense coat of hairs that were about a quarter inch (6 millimeters) long.[6] Artists were quick to acknowledge this theory, and pretty soon many books were featuring paintings of furry pterosaurs of all kinds.

As interesting as this theory was, nothing like hair had ever been seen before in a pterosaur. About twenty-four years later, in 1994, two specialists in pterosaur flight took a closer look at the supposedly hairy wings of *Sordes*. Paleontologists David Unwin and Natasha Bakhurina showed that the traces seen in the *Sordes* specimen were not hair at all, but stiffening fibers that gave strength to the wings.[7] These same fibrous elements have also been seen in other pterosaurs. So the "hairy devil" *Sordes* was not so hairy after all.

This does not mean that pterosaurs did not have some hair for insulation. There is compelling evidence on a specimen of *Rhamphorhynchus* for hairy fibers on the neck and limbs, but most paleontologists are reluctant to support the theory of hairy pterosaurs until other specimens of flying reptiles show the same kinds of traces.[8]

The pigment of pterosaur skin and hair did not fossilize, so scientists can only guess at the color of these creatures. One can guess that pterosaur body color varied widely, as color does in today's reptiles and birds. Color may have played an important role in telling the difference between males and females of the species, and as a means for attracting a mate.

Wings

The wings of all pterosaurs were remarkably similar through-out their 160-million-year reign. Pterosaurs had a relatively short but muscular forearm with three clawed fingers of normal length. The fourth finger, however, was greatly elongated to form the front edge of the wing. It consisted of four bones locked together to form a stiff frame.

The leathery wing membrane extended from the side of the pterosaur and was stretched by the bones of the forearm and fourth finger when extended. The wing had two sections. The forewing was a small patch of wing that stretched between the animal's wrist and its side. The main part of the wing extended from its side and was attached to the length of the forearm all the way to the tip of the fourth finger. The wing was flexible enough to be folded close to the body when the animal was on the ground and at rest.

Some of the small rhamphorhynchoids such as *Dimorphodon* and *Sordes* had a pronounced wing membrane between their hind legs and tail. Most other pterosaurs,

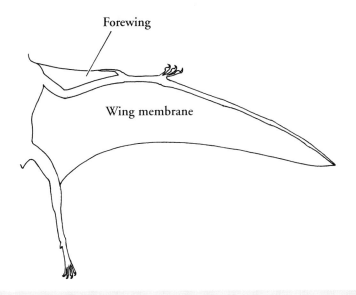

Forewing

Wing membrane

Pterosaur wings were formed by the elongated fourth finger of the hand and covered with a leathery membrane.

especially the short-tailed kinds, did not have a membrane between their legs, but the wings often extended down the top of the legs to the knee.

Pterosaur wings were flexible yet quite strong. The skin-like wing membrane was strengthened by a parallel pattern of internal stiffening fibers. These fibers were about the width of a thread and packed close together in rows, about one hundred per inch. These fibers were probably made of keratin, the same material that makes up fingernails, horns, and claws.

Scientists can tell that pterosaur wings were designed for powered flight by examining how the bones of the wings fit together. There are places on the bones where muscles were

This drawing of the small pterosaur Sordes shows a body covered with fine hair. Although the evidence for a hairy coat on this particular pterosaur has now been disputed, evidence for hair on other small pterosaurs has been found in fossils. Sordes also had a long wing membrane stretched between its legs. This was not seen in short-tailed pterosaurs.

attached. Comparisons can be made to the bones of birds and bats to see how the wings of pterosaurs were like today's flying vertebrates. Powered flight requires wings that can flap in a wide cycle from upstroke to downstroke. Pterosaurs clearly had the skeletal structures and muscles capable of this kind of motion.

As mentioned earlier, flight can consist of powered flapping, gliding, and soaring. The design of the wing and supporting skeletal structure determines which is possible. The early long-tailed pterosaurs had short, broad wings, indicating that they were active flappers but somewhat less stable in the air than their descendents. The long tail of the early rhamphorhynchoids helped stabilize their flight. Later rhamphorhynchoids developed long, narrow wings that were more suited for soaring.

The small, short-tailed pterodactyloids were also active flappers. The largest pterosaurs, such as *Pteranodon*, had long, narrow wings and were well adapted for gliding, soaring, and powered flight. *Pteranodon* was so lightweight for its large wingspan that it is likely it could have stayed aloft for long periods, riding updrafts and soaring for perhaps a hundred miles or more.

Another anatomical feature affecting flight was the tail flap seen in some of the long-tailed pterosaurs. The flap usually had a rounded diamond shape and was positioned vertically. It was used in the air like the rudder of a boat to stabilize and help maneuver the animal in flight.

Freaky Beaks and Curious Crests– The Pterosaur Skull

Pterosaurs possessed some of the most bizarre skulls ever found in nature. The skull is the one part of the skeleton that clearly separates one kind of pterosaur from another. It is what gives them personality. There is the devilish snarl of *Rhamphorhynchus*, the toothy grin of *Ornithodesmus* ("bird ribbon"), and the peaceable, puzzled look of the filter feeder *Pterodaustro* ("southern wing"). The skull also tells a story about how these creatures fended for themselves in getting food, providing vivid mental pictures of the lifestyles of these fascinating flyers.

Pterosaur skulls vary widely from one family to another. One thing that is common among all flying reptiles is that the skull was oversized when compared to the rest of the body. It was probably just heavy enough to serve as a counterbalance to the torso so that the animal could fly in a stable manner. Some also had long tails and large head crests to further improve stability during flight.

The shapes of pterosaur skulls varied widely, especially the jaws. A few of the small rhamphorhynchoids had tall, rounded, boxlike skulls with short jaws and nostrils on the front of the snout. The most typical pterosaur skull shape is the long and narrow variety seen in many rhamphorhynchoids and pterodactyloids. These were slim and pointed, had nostrils closer to the eyes, and usually had a dazzling array of pointed teeth for snagging fish. Several others had jaws that were

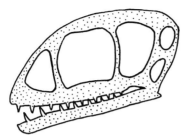

Anurognathus

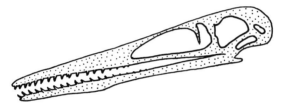

Pterodactylus

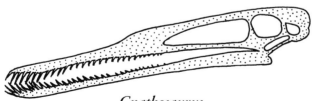

Gnathosaurus

There is variation in the skulls of different pterosaurs.

unique even among the pterosaurs. Filter feeders such as *Gnathosaurus* ("jaw lizard") had extraordinarily long and narrow jaws that were outlined with a thick comb of long, thin teeth. These "basket feeders" would swish their mouths through the water to catch small sea creatures in their teeth. You may read more about pterosaur teeth and other unusual feeding adaptations of the pterosaurs in Chapter 6.

In addition to their wildly different jaw designs, many pterosaurs were adorned with bony crests on their heads. These head crests seem to have had two functions. One was that of visual display. Crests were a way to attract the attention of potential mates. Perhaps the largest and most decorative frills were viewed as belonging to the most desirable mates.

The other function was that of flight stabilization. Several kinds of pterosaur frills were prominent enough to have affected the aerodynamics of the animal's flight.

Crests came in several varieties. One common type was a short bony ridge running up the center of the nose, a feature that is seen in many rhamphorhynchoids and pterodactyloids. The purpose of this crest was most certainly for visual display and may have varied in size between males and females. It was probably not prominent enough to have aided the creature in flight.

Crests on the back of the head were found on many of the pterodactyloids. These ranged in size from a small bump like that on the back of the skull of *Gallodactylus* ("Gallic finger") to the long and stunning crests of *Pteranodon*. The latter had two basic crest shapes, each found on different species. One

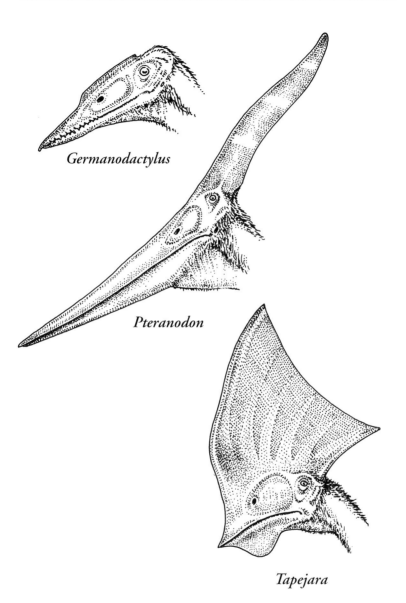

Germanodactylus

Pteranodon

Tapejara

Pterosaur crests were sometimes a short bony ridge, as in Germanodactylus. Other times it was on the back of the head, such as the long crest of Pteranodon.

was long and pointed and stretched out behind the head nearly as long as the beak stretched out in front. The other was a wide, hatchet-shaped crest positioned on the cap of the skull over the eyes. These large crests certainly affected the animal's ability to maneuver in the air, acting as a kind of rudder for steering and also as a counterbalance to the heavy beak. There is also evidence that the size of the crest may have differed between males and females, providing a clear visual cue as to who was who during mating season.

Pteranodon skulls

A third variety of head crest is perhaps the most remarkable of all. Several kinds of pterosaurs sported a pair of large, rounded crests at the front of the jaws. One was on top of the snout, the other below. These semicircular vanes nearly formed a circle when the jaws were closed. It is believed that the pterosaur could dip this crest into the water when it was skimming the sea for food, stabilizing its flight and allowing it to use the water as a medium for changing direction. One could liken this to the action of an oar in the water. *Anhanguera* ("old devil") and *Tropeognathus* ("keel jaw") each had crests of this variety.

Even with their remarkable jaws and crests, the skulls of pterosaurs were still designed for lightness and strength. They often had hollow pockets where bone was not needed. The

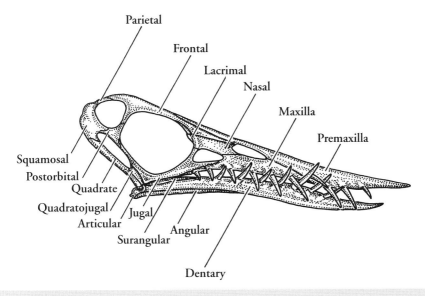

The skull of Rhamphorhynchus

bony walls for the mouth, nostril, eye, and ear chambers were thin but reinforced the overall sturdiness of the skull.

Anatomy of the Rhamphorhynchus Skull

Skulls are composed of many small parts. Each part has its own name. Most of these parts are found in all pterosaur skulls, but they vary in size and shape depending on the particular kind of flying reptile. Pterosaur skulls are often found in fragments, making it important for the paleontologist to be able to recognize these creatures from the smallest of pieces. The elements found in the skull of a large pterosaur are illustrated here using *Rhamphorhynchus*.

CHAPTER 4

LIFESTYLE AND PHYSIOLOGY OF THE FLYING REPTILES

Physiology is the study of how a body operates. The physiology of pterosaurs is understood by comparing the evidence from fossils to the anatomy and physiology of today's creatures. Other physical evidence, such as fossilized footprints, has also been used to piece together theories about the behavior and movement of pterosaurs.

The Pterosaur Brain

The pterosaur brain, like other soft tissues and organs, has not been preserved in the fossil record. However, the approximate size of a pterosaur's brain can be determined by making a cast of the brain cavity, or braincase, in the skull. Most pterosaur skull material is too incomplete to include an undamaged braincase. However, it has been possible to make brain casts from a select few pterosaurs, including specimens of *Rhamphorhynchus, Pterodactylus,* and *Pteranodon.* These casts have led to some surprising information about pterosaurs.

The braincase in a pterosaur skull holds clues to the many connections between the brain and other parts of the body. Evidence of nerve connections can be seen in the form of holes in the braincase through which nerves were once threaded to attach the brain to other organs.

The brains of modern vertebrates—particularly those of reptiles and birds—are similar in many ways. The sense of smell is located at the front of the brain in the olfactory lobe. Vision is concentrated in an optic lobe found on both sides of the brain. Observing the kinds of nerve connections that exist in today's animals can help a paleontologist identify the locations of similar features in the skulls of extinct vertebrates.

One of the first scientists to study the structure of brains in extinct creatures was Tilly Edinger. She was the founder of modern paleoneurology. In 1927 she published an important study of the brains of pterosaurs based on several casts of their brain cavities. She discovered that pterosaurs had brains that were more like those of birds than of reptiles. This was surprising because pterosaurs, like the dinosaurs, evolved from early reptiles. Yet their brains were more like those of birds in their general size, shape, and orientation. The brains of pterosaurs from the Late Jurassic Period were even more like those of modern birds than of *Archaeopteryx*, the first bird, which lived at the same time.[1] These conclusions have been recently reaffirmed by paleontologist Deborah S. Wharton, who has been comparing the brains of dinosaurs, birds, and pterosaurs. Wharton also concludes that pterosaurs may have had brains as well developed as those of modern birds.[2]

One of the most striking differences between pterosaur brains and those of other reptiles is that they have greatly enlarged optic lobes. This makes sense, because a flying creature that must swoop down and snatch up its prey must have superior eyesight. The idea that pterosaurs had keen eyesight is also supported by the fact that their eyes were large.

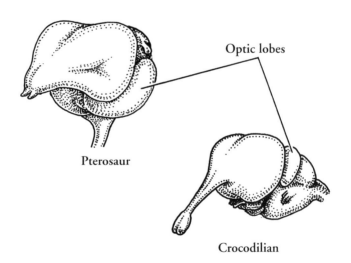

The optic lobes of the pterosaur brain are clearly larger than those of their crocodile relatives. This is a sign of a keen sense of eyesight, which would help the flying predator catch its next meal.

How did the pterosaurs evolve a birdlike brain long before the appearance of true birds? Probably because they lived a similar lifestyle. Predatory creatures rely on their senses to locate and catch prey. Animals that fly develop superior senses of balance and vision. The parts of the brain devoted to controlling these abilities, along with steering and maneuvering, were more developed in pterosaur brains than in those of crocodiles, dinosaurs, and other reptiles. The bird brain evolved in a similar way, emphasizing the development of those parts of the brain devoted to flight, vision, and balance.

How intelligent was a pterosaur? To understand how this can be known, one needs to understand how the size of the brain can be used to measure an animal's "smarts."

The intelligence of extinct creatures can never be proven. After all, what is intelligence? Intelligence can be described as the ability to process information, or to learn. Since this is something we will never be able to observe in pterosaurs, we must rely on other clues to intelligence that are found in the fossil record. Chief among these is the size of the animal's brain in proportion to the size of its body.

In examining many kinds of living animals, scientists have found a relationship between the size of the brain and the size of a creature's body. A species whose brain is larger than expected for its body size is considered more intelligent. This allows a comparison of the intelligence of animals of different body sizes, say a Pekingese dog with an Irish wolfhound. By this measure, mammals and birds are considered to be more intelligent than fish, amphibians, and reptiles. What makes humans so unusual is that our brain size is seven times greater than should be expected for a creature with our body size.

The size of a pterosaur's brain compared to its body size suggests that pterosaurs were about as intelligent as an average bird. This is indirectly supported by the assumption that they had birdlike lives in hunting, nesting, and even brooding their young, although there is no direct fossil evidence to support some of these behaviors without question. Based on these assumptions, pterosaurs were near the top of the class of Mesozoic intelligence when compared to early birds, crocodiles, and plant-eating dinosaurs.

Growth Rate

What can the fossil record tell us about how fast the pterosaurs grew from hatchling to adult? Paleontologists base their understanding of the growth rates of extinct animals on their knowledge of growth in modern reptiles, birds, and other animals. Knowledge about reptile and bird growth is abundant. Unlike birds and mammals, which reach a peak size soon after reaching sexual maturity, reptiles continue to grow throughout their lives. Their rate of growth slows considerably after reaching sexual maturity, but they continue to grow nonetheless.

Additional clues to the growth rate of extinct animals come from studying their bones under a microscope. A magnified cross section of bone reveals the bone's cellular structure. At one extreme, some bones formed in a smooth, continuous pattern. This indicates that the animal was growing continuously and steadily, perhaps rapidly. At the other extreme, some bone tissue formed with curious rings called lines of arrested growth. These growth rings are much like the seasonal rings in cross sections of tree trunks. This phenomenon is also seen in the bones of modern reptiles. It represents an annual period when growth slows down, perhaps during a cool season when the animal is less active. The bones of pterosaurs reveal few if any lines of arrested growth, suggesting that pterosaurs grew rapidly and at a continuous rate.[3]

Were pterosaurs more like reptiles or birds? It appears that they were more like birds and probably grew quite rapidly in the early stages of life. Like birds, they probably stopped growing after reaching sexual maturity. Otherwise, if they continued to get bigger and bigger, their increased size could have eventually inhibited their ability to fly.[4]

Were Pterosaurs Warm-Blooded?

The question of body temperature has been a source of lively debate in the study of dinosaurs. There is more agreement among scientists, however, when it comes to the flying reptiles. From the earliest days of pterosaur study, scientists have believed that these creatures were endotherms (warm-blooded), not ectotherms (cold-blooded). Warm-blooded creatures have an internal source of body heat regulated by their heart and circulatory system. They are not dependent on the environment as their source of heat and can remain physically active for sustained periods of time. Cold-blooded creatures have a simpler heart, and their body temperature is regulated by the temperature around them. They generally exert energy in shorter bursts and are less active, spending much of their time basking in the sun to maintain a safe body temperature.

Harry Govier Seeley was one of the first great paleontologists to conduct a thorough study of pterosaurs. In 1864 he stated that the flying reptiles were probably warm-blooded.[5] He based his conclusion on the fact that a pterosaur's blood temperature would rise simply when the creature flapped its wings. This seems like a reasonable conclusion, because it requires much energy to sustain powered flight. To stay aloft, a flying creature might have to keep flapping for a long time. Birds and bats are both warm-blooded creatures. It is difficult to imagine an active flying creature that was cold-blooded, because it would not be able to stay in the air very long. It would not be able to take in heat energy from the surrounding environment quickly enough to keep up with the energy it spent by flapping its wings.

The idea that pterosaurs were warm-blooded is supported by several other pieces of indirect evidence. Their bones show that pterosaurs grew continuously and rapidly, much like today's warm-blooded birds. Pterosaurs also may have been covered with a coat of hair. Hair serves as protection from the cold and is found today only on warm-blooded creatures. The feathers of birds, too, are thought to have had origins in hair-like filaments.

Perhaps one of the strongest pieces of indirect evidence that flying reptiles were warm-blooded has to do with their hollow bones. Like birds, it appears that pterosaurs had a sophisticated network of air sacs connected to their lungs. The air sacs branched throughout the body and even occupied spaces in the hollows of some bones. This has two immediate benefits for a warm-blooded bird or pterosaur. First, it allows ventilating air to circulate throughout the body and keep it cool. Overexertion and overheating are problems for birds and must have been for pterosaurs as well. Second, by recirculating air from the lungs through the bones and back to the lungs again, more oxygen can be absorbed from the air. Muscles need oxygen to work properly, so this respiratory system of air sacs helps make the most use of the air that the animal breathes in.

Walking

There is no question that pterosaurs were built for flying and not for efficient walking. However, two lines of thought have evolved regarding the movement of pterosaurs on the ground.

It was originally thought that pterosaurs crawled on all fours, wing arms outstretched, dragging their bellies like bats, creeping along ever so slowly. This was the accepted view for many years. Some scientists thought that pterosaurs were virtually helpless while on the ground and often pictured them hanging upside down or clinging from cliffs instead. A modern interpretation of the pterosaur skeleton by paleontologist Peter Wellnhofer suggests that instead of dragging their bellies, pterosaurs may have raised themselves up on the knuckles of the three clawed fingers on their forearms. In this position, the wing would have been bent backward at the joint of the fourth

Most paleontologists believe that pterosaurs could walk on all fours.

finger. This would have allowed them to clear the ground and guardedly waddle on all fours.[6]

Another theory is that pterosaurs walked upright on their hind legs, much as birds do today. This was originally proposed as a way to explain how pterosaurs could take off from the ground: They would get a running start before gaining wing speed.[7] A more recent study by Kevin Padian of the pterosaur *Dimorphodon* led him to a similar conclusion that all pterosaurs could walk on two legs like birds.

While the two-legged view is attractive and makes pterosaurs even more birdlike, the widely accepted view today is that pterosaurs walked on all fours. There are several reasons for this, mostly having to do with the anatomy of the hips and wings. Unlike birds, which have an upright standing posture, the hip sockets of the pterosaurs were oriented sideways, more like a lizard's. This means that the legs were attached so that they jutted out to the sides somewhat and were not positioned directly under the body as in birds. In addition, in order for a pterosaur to maintain a balanced upright posture while standing, its wings would have had to be able to fold against its body. This was not possible in pterosaurs. The wing could fold at only one place—the joint where the elongated fourth finger was attached. The combination of sprawling legs with outstretched wings would have made it very difficult for a pterosaur to maintain balance while standing on two legs. Finally, the fact that the pterosaur foot was not built like those of good runners adds further credibility to the walking-on-all-fours theory.

Fossilized footprints of dinosaurs, called trackways, have been found in many parts of the world. They have enabled paleontologists to better understand how dinosaurs walked and how fast they could move. Trackways of pterosaurs could be similarly used to confirm just how they walked. But fossilized footprints of pterosaurs are rare. It would seem that their high-flying lifestyle greatly reduced the possibility that they would leave many footprints behind. This makes sense because they probably perched on rocky cliffs and trees, where footprints could not be made. Any footsteps left by pterosaurs on the beach would soon have been washed away.

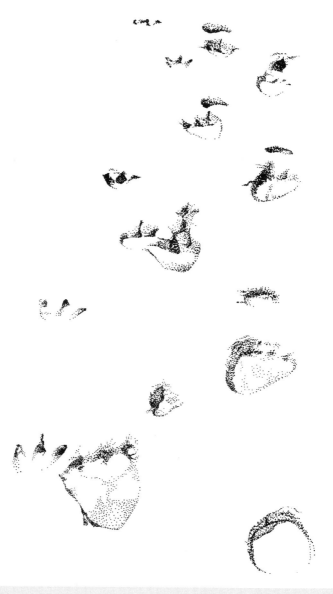

Fossilized footprints of dinosaurs, such as these found in Dinosaur State Park, Texas, are called trackways. These show the paths of meat-eating (left) and plant-eating (right) dinosaurs. Fossilized footprints of pterosaurs are rare.

Trackway experts Martin Lockley and Adrian Hunt have recently reported that as many as four pterosaur track sites have now been found. Not all of these are accepted by other scientists as being made by pterosaurs, however, so there is still some debate about the validity of these tracks. The most promising set was found in Late Jurassic deposits of Wyoming that were once part of a salty lagoon, an ideal place to capture the footprints of a pterosaur. The tracks show that the pterosaur was walking on all fours. The rear feet closely match the size and shape of known pterosaurs from the same region.[8] The animal seems to be raised up on the sides of its hand claws, similar to how Wellnhofer had pictured it, so that its belly did not drag. While this evidence is not accepted by everyone, it furthers the theory that pterosaurs indeed walked on all fours.

Males and Females

Telling the males from the females is not easy from skeletons. Paleontologists can be comfortable about doing this only when an abundance of skeletons from the same kind of dinosaur can be compared. They look for differences that could distinguish the males from the females. These traits are the result of sexual dimorphism—naturally occurring differences between the sexes of the same kind of animal. These differences may be in size, shape, or behavior. In nature, they often help members of the species identify the males from the females, and they may also have other important functions. For example, male elephants have tusks that are used during combat or jousting with other males. Male deer have antlers to lock and wrestle with rivals to win the favor of females.

In the fossils of some kinds of dinosaurs, there are obvious differences that suggest which ones are males and females. For example, the size and showiness of the frill of the horned dinosaur *Protoceratops* ("first horned face") probably distinguished males from females.[9] Crested duck-billed

Protoceratops

dinosaurs are another species for which abundant skeletal specimens provide clues to separating the males from females. *Corythosaurus* ("helmet lizard"), *Lambeosaurus* ("Lambe's lizard), and *Parasaurolophus* ("near *Saurolophus*") are all examples of duck-billed dinosaurs whose

Corythosaurus

skulls show two distinctly different crest shapes as a result of variation between the males and females.

In the study of pterosaurs, there are several cases that provide good clues as to differ-

Lambeosaurus

ences between males and females. The first comes from a study of the many specimens of *Rhamphorhynchus* that have been discovered in Solnhofen. One species of this animal shows up in the fossil record in two forms: One has a long skull and wide wingspan, the other has a shorter skull and shorter wingspan.[10] It can be presumed that this represents a difference between males and females of the same species, although which is which is still a matter of speculation. The accepted view is that the larger variety is the male.[11]

Another intriguing case is based on skeletal differences in specimens of *Pteranodon*. One form of the same species is larger than the other and has a larger head crest but a smaller opening in the hip. The smaller form with the larger pelvic opening is thought to be the female.[12] The larger opening in the pelvis is interpreted to be the canal by which the female lays her eggs.

Based on this evidence, it is fair to assume that differences in the size and shape of the head crest in pterosaurs of the same species was usually a visual marker that distinguished the males from the females.

CHAPTER 5

EGGS AND BABIES

There is no undisputed evidence of pterosaur eggs and embryos. While it might be remotely possible that they gave birth to live young, the prevailing opinion in paleontology is that pterosaurs laid eggs in nests, like birds. Unfortunately, no one has ever found a fossilized pterosaur nest with eggs in it, so most of what is believed about this subject is based on the educated guesses of scientists. And intriguing guesses they are!

Assuming that pterosaurs laid eggs, what were the eggs like? The pelvic canal through which the eggs would have passed was not very large, so it is assumed that the eggs were equally small. In proportion to body size, the eggs were probably closer to the size of birds' eggs than reptilian eggs. Pterosaurs probably did not lay very many eggs, either; the weight of carrying them in the body would have inhibited flight.[1] Perhaps they laid only two or three eggs at a time, like many birds today.

Being warm-blooded creatures, another assumption is that pterosaur eggs needed to stay warm so that they would incubate. This might have been accomplished simply by having a nest that was in the sunshine. The heat of the sun combined with the moist, warm air of the semitropical Mesozoic climate could have been plenty to keep the eggs warm.

It has also been suggested that the female pterosaur may have brooded or sat on her eggs until they hatched. This bird-like scenario also suggests that the mate of the female pterosaur may have brought food to the nest for the mother to eat.

Specimens of young pterosaurs have been discovered, and they show that they probably could not fly at birth. This suggests the intriguing possibility that pterosaur parents cared for their nestlings the same way that modern birds do. It was presumably the job of the female to retrieve food and give it to her hatchlings.

Even though nesting sites for pterosaurs have not yet been discovered, there is reason to believe that pterosaurs may have created vast colonies of nests high out of reach of predators. This would be similar to the kind of social behavior found in some birds, such as gulls and pelicans, and suggests a sophisticated level of intelligence. One can imagine a cliff overlooking the crashing waves of an ocean far below, with dozens, maybe hundreds, of pterosaurs in a vast colony tending their young.

CHAPTER 6

FEEDING HABITS AND ADAPTATIONS

One needs only to look at the long, toothy jaws of the typical pterosaur to understand its eating habits. The jaws were key when it came to catching and gobbling down prey. Even though pterosaurs had three clawed fingers on their forelimbs, it is unlikely that these were used to grasp or grapple prey. Instead, it is assumed from their anatomy that pterosaurs swooped down from the sky to snatch their prey from the sea or land using their specialized jaws.

The fact that most pterosaur specimens have been found in environments that were once aquatic has led scientists to conclude that pterosaurs were mostly fish eaters. This has been confirmed by the remains of meals that have been found in the stomach area of several pterosaur fossils. This is not to say that a pterosaur might not have snatched up a small lizard or mammal once in a while. But fish were available in abundance and were probably easy pickings for the sharp-eyed pterosaurs.

One kind of fish that has been found in the stomach contents of fossilized pterosaurs is the herringlike *Leptolepis*, a small fish that moved in large schools.[1] Fossils of this fish have been found in the same geographic areas as many pterosaurs, including Europe, North America, Australia, and Tanzania. It lived from the Middle Triassic to Early Cretaceous Periods. Other fishy meals for the pterosaurs may have included the ray-finned *Thrissops, Protobrama,* and *Pholidophorus;* the salmon-ancestor *Sphenocephalus;* and the early ray-finned *Lepidotes.* These fish ranged in length from about 6 inches to 2 feet (15 to 60 centimeters).

The long-jawed pterosaurs had teeth that were well adapted for fishing expeditions. The flying reptiles had some of the most elaborate and bizarre teeth adaptations that have ever been seen. Not all were fish eaters, however. A few small species with short, rounded skulls were better adapted at snapping large Mesozoic insects than diving at the water for a taste of seafood.

Following is a roundup of the many kinds of jaw designs and teeth that have been found in pterosaurs.

Short, widely spaced, pointed teeth. The teeth in the front of the jaws were usually longer than those in back, enabling the pterosaur to spear fish as it flew over the water. The teeth of the upper and lower jaws might also mesh or interlock when the jaws were closed, providing a firm grip on the prey. Examples of pterosaurs with these teeth include *Eudimorphodon, Dimorphodon, Ornithocheirus,* and *Ornithodesmus.*

Long, angled, widely spaced, needlelike teeth. The front teeth were often long and curved, pointing forward outside of the mouth. Smaller teeth were in the back of the jaws. The front teeth were well suited for spearing large fish. Examples of pterosaurs with these teeth include *Rhamphorhynchus* and *Scaphognathus.*

Peglike, widely spaced teeth and a short, wide jaw. These were best suited for eating insects and were generally not angled forward. The teeth of the upper and lower jaws would interlock when the mouth was closed. Examples include *Sordes* and *Anurognathus* ("tailless jaw").

Long and short pointed teeth. The teeth in the front were longer than those in the back and were angled forward. They were spaced so that they interlocked when the jaws were closed, an advantage for grasping large fish. With a mouth full of teeth, the pterosaur could skim the water to scoop up its prey with ease. Examples include *Pterodactylus* and *Germanodactylus* ("German finger").

Long, closely spaced teeth in the front of the jaws. These were used for spearing fish with a jabbing strike into the water. Some had smaller teeth in the back of the mouth. Examples of pterosaurs with these teeth include *Gallodactylus* and *Cearadactylus* ("Ceará [Brazil] finger").

Filterlike basket of teeth. Several pterosaurs had this unusual adaptation on either their lower jaw or both the upper and lower jaws. Long, tightly packed, needlelike teeth around the edge of the mouth acted as a kind of basket. It is unlikely that these creatures fed while they were flying, because the force would have damaged their teeth. These pterosaurs probably stood in the shallow water like flamingos, bending down to scoop up water in their mouths. By filling its mouth with water, the pterosaur could filter out any small creatures, such as plankton. Examples include *Ctenochasma* ("comb jaws"), *Gnathosaurus,* and *Pterodaustro.*

Long, pointed beak with short, pointed teeth in the back of the jaw. This kind of pterosaur may have used its beak to pry open shellfish. Examples of pterosaurs with these teeth include *Dsungaripterus* ("Junggar Basin wing"), *Noripterus* ("lake wing"), and *Phobetor* ("frightening one").

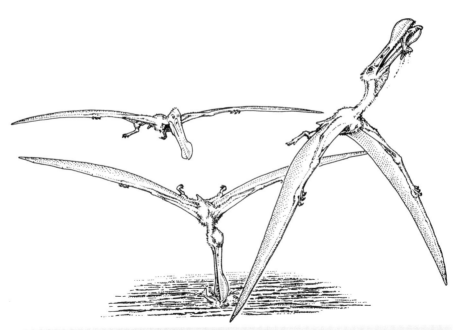

Tropeognathus had rounded crests on the front of its jaw. This helped it during its hunting for food in the water.

Crested, rudderlike jaws and pointed teeth. These pterosaurs had a mouthful of pointed teeth and a rounded crest on the outside of the top and bottom jaws. When the pterosaur was flying over the water, it could use its rudderlike crested jaws to steady its flight. Examples include *Criorhynchus* ("ram snout") and *Tropeognathus.*

Long pointed jaws without teeth. Some of the larger pterosaurs had no teeth, using their pointed jaws to grab fish and swallow them whole. Examples include *Pteranodon, Ornithostoma* ("bird mouth"), and *Quetzalcoatlus.*

The fossilized teeth of adult pterosaurs often show wear. This was probably from the pterosaur having chewed on the tough armor plating of some of the fish that were common at the time. Younger pterosaur specimens do not show such tooth wear. This indicates that they may have fed on something softer, such as insects.[2]

Being a fish eater sometimes had it dangers. Fish get hungry, too. There is evidence that a large predatory fish once got the better of a small rhamphorhynchoid pterosaur named *Preondactylus* ("Preone finger"). As the pterosaur was skimming the waves for a small fish to catch, a large, hungry fish called *Saurichthys* ("lizard fish") leaped from the water and clamped down on the pterosaur with its jaws. The pterosaur soon became fish food. The fish evidently could not digest all of *Preondactylus'* bones, so it vomited them in the form of a pellet. This pellet became fossilized for scientists to discover 200 million years later.

Not all pterosaurs have been found where there was

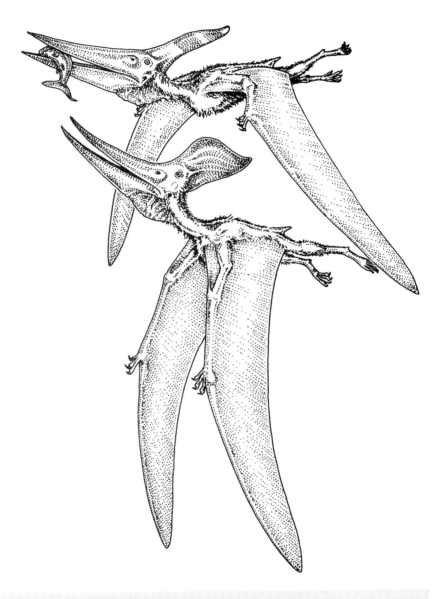

Pteranodon used their pointed jaws to grab fish.

seawater. It appears that the largest kinds of flying reptiles, such as *Quetzalcoatlus,* may have lived inland. If they did, what did they eat? It is possible that they scooped up fish from freshwater ponds. Some scientists also suggest that they may have been scavengers—giant reptilian vultures.[3] Imagine a *Quetzalcoatlus* poking around inside a carcass with its long beak. But without teeth, it may have had difficulty cutting off chunks of flesh to swallow. Without further evidence, the vision of a vulturelike *Quetzalcoatlus* is difficult for most paleontologists to accept.

CHAPTER 7

EXTINCTION OF THE PTEROSAURS

Pterosaurs were most plentiful during the Late Jurassic Period and the first half of the Cretaceous Period. The long-tailed rhamphorhynchoids were masters of the Jurassic airways. During the Early Cretaceous Period, they were evidently squeezed out by the short-tailed and more agile pterodactyloids that followed them. By the middle part of the Cretaceous, only the pterodactyloids remained. The smaller members of this group gradually became extinct, leaving only the largest forms, the azhdarchids, to fly the skies during the final days of the dinosaurs. Competition from birds—which first became abundant during the Early Cretaceous—may have contributed to the demise of the smaller pterosaurs.

Along with dinosaurs, pterosaurs were one of the most successful forms of life ever to inhabit our planet. Their existence lasted for 160 million years. By comparison, humans and even our most distant relatives have been around for only about 4 million years.

Although the pterosaurs existed for so many millions of years, most species existed for only a few million years at a time, until they became extinct or evolved into "improved" versions that adapted to changes in the environment. So, to say that all the pterosaurs became extinct at the end of the Cretaceous Period is incorrect—most kinds of pterosaurs had already come and gone by then. There is no denying, though, that a mass extinction occurred at the end of the Cretaceous that wiped out about 65 to 70 percent of all animal life, including the dinosaurs, pterosaurs, and marine reptiles. Even the groups of animals that survived—including frogs, lizards, turtles, salamanders, birds, insects, fish, crocodiles, alligators, and mammals—lost great numbers of their species.

Chief among the causes of animal extinction are environmental changes that affect their food supply or body chemistry (such as sustained changes in climatic temperature), disease, and natural disasters (such as volcanic eruptions, earthquakes, and the changing surface of Earth). Extensive hunting by natural enemies may also contribute to extinction. Humankind, for example, has hunted many animals such as the buffalo to extinction or near extinction.

Why did the last of the pterosaurs and the dinosaurs become extinct? This is a great mystery of science. Any suitable explanation must account for the disappearance of pterosaurs, dinosaurs, reptiles that swam in the oceans, ammonites, and other sea creatures, including some types of clams, mollusks, and plankton. One must also explain why so many other types of animals continued to thrive after this mass extinction.

Paleontologists disagree on the exact cause of the extinctions at the end of the Cretaceous Period and the length of time it took for this mass dying to occur. There are many theories about what happened. They come in two basic varieties: gradual causes and sudden causes.

Gradual causes would have required millions of years of change. Some possible gradual causes include global climate changes (warming or cooling), volcanic action, shifting of continents, overpopulation, and the appearance of egg-stealing mammals.

Sudden or catastrophic causes would have taken no longer than a few years to wipe out the pterosaurs. One of the most popular extinction theories concerns the collision of an asteroid or comet with Earth.

So far, no single extinction theory can fully explain the great dying at the end of the age of dinosaurs. Evidence has been mounting in favor of the asteroid theory. But a collision with an asteroid may have only been the final blow in a gradual extinction that had been growing for many years. The asteroid theory also fails to explain why the extinction was so selective. Why did marine reptiles die but most fish survive? Why did pterosaurs and dinosaurs of all sizes disappear but birds and mammals continue to thrive? There are still many questions to answer before we totally understand this great mystery.

The fact that they are extinct adds to our fascination with the pterosaurs. Flying reptiles now exist only in fantasies and fairy tales about brave warriors doing battle with fire-breathing dragons. But there once was a time on this planet when flying reptiles did truly master the skies, and all that lived in their shadow took notice.

CHAPTER 8

MAJOR PTEROSAUR DISCOVERIES

This chapter summarizes the major discoveries of pterosaurs. It chronicles the most important and complete specimens that have been discovered, when and where they were found, and the people who identified them.

✦ ✦ ✦

1784 (Germany)—The first description of a pterosaur fossil was published by naturalist **Cosimo Alessandro Collini**. The German specimen, found in Eichstätt, was discovered in the exquisite limestone deposits of Bavaria, most likely from the Solnhofen region known for the later discovery of *Archaeopteryx* (1861), the first bird. This small creature puzzled Collini. It had a skull with a long, toothed snout and a wingspan of about 3 feet (1 meter). He could not classify it as a bird, mammal, reptile, or other known kind of vertebrate.

✦ ✦ ✦

1812 (France)—Since its discovery, the 1784 Eichstätt pterosaur specimen had been variously described by different naturalists as anything from a waterbird to a bat. French anatomist **Georges Cuvier**, known as the father of vertebrate paleontology, was the first to accurately describe this specimen as a special kind of reptile, which he called *Pterodactylus* ("wing finger"), the first known pterosaur. It dated from the Late Jurassic Period. This pterosaur had a short tail, making it the first described

Pterodactylus

member of the group of pterosaurs called Pterodactyloidea.

✦ ✦ ✦

1833 (Germany)—Another extraordinary find in the Bavarian Solnhofen limestone revealed the small lower jaw of one of the strangest of all pterosaurs, *Gnathosaurus* ("jaw lizard"). The specimen was mistaken for part of a crocodile jaw and named by paleontologist **Hermann von Meyer**. It wasn't until a more complete skull was discovered in 1951 that this creature was correctly identified as another kind of pterosaur. It had a long, narrow jaw with lengthy teeth lining the outer edges of the jawline. The teeth were used for filtering out small prey from the sea. It lived during the Late Jurassic Period.

1839 (Germany)—Until this time, all previously recognized pterosaur specimens lacked teeth and had only short tails. The first evidence of a second kind of pterosaur with a long tail and teeth was discovered at Solnhofen and described by **Graf Münster** as *Pterodactylus longicaudus*, the long-tailed *Pterodactylus*. The name was later changed to *Rhamphorhynchus longicaudus* when the specimen was placed in the group of pterosaurs known as the Rhamphorhynchoidea. It dated from the Late Jurassic Period.

1847 (Germany)—Hermann von Meyer described *Rhamphorhynchus* ("beak snout"), a small, toothed pterosaur with a long tail. The Rhamphorhynchoidea, one of the two main groups of pterosaurs, was named after this creature. It is one of the most plentiful pterosaurs found at Solnhofen and is represented by five species of various sizes. It lived during the Late Jurassic Period in Europe.

✦ ✦ ✦

1852 (Germany)—A pterosaur with a bizarre tooth array was named by **Hermann von Meyer**. *Ctenochasma* ("comb jaws") had a long snout and narrow jaw. Its mouth was adapted for filter feeding using a dense comb of needlelike teeth. *Ctenochasma* lived during the Late Jurassic Period. A similar jaw style of the filter-feeding *Gnathosaurus* was discovered in 1833, but it was not recognized as a pterosaur until 1951.

1859 (England)—*Dimorphodon* ("two-form tooth") was discovered and named by British comparative anatomist **Richard Owen**. It was relatively small, with a 4-foot (1.2-meter) wingspan. Its head was tall and narrow and shaped more like that of a bird than other members of the rhamphorhynchoids. It lived during the Early Jurassic Period.

Dimorphodon

1861 (Germany)—Discovered in the Solnhofen limestone, *Scaphognathus* ("boat jaw") was a small rhamphorhynchoid similar to *Rhamphorhynchus*. It differed in that it had longer teeth that were set in an upright position rather than being pointed forward and outward as in *Rhamphorhynchus*. *Scaphognathus* was named by **Andreas Wagner**.

Scaphognathus

1869 (England)—*Ornithocheirus* ("bird hand") was a mid-sized, short-tailed pterosaur with upright teeth set in a long tapering jaw. It is one of the most commonly found pterosaur fossils from the Late Cretaceous Period. It was named by **Harry Govier Seeley**.

Ornithocheirus

1876 (United States)—Othniel Charles Marsh, one of America's foremost dinosaur hunters of the nineteenth century, also discovered some important pterosaur remains. The most familiar is *Pteranodon* ("toothless flyer"), a large toothless variety from the Late Cretaceous Period. It had a

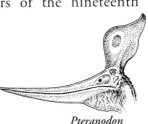

Pteranodon

magnificent head crest. Some species had a wingspan of 30 feet (9 meters).

✦ ✦ ✦

1923 (Germany)—*Anurognathus* ("tailless jaw") was named by **Doederline**. This small rhamphorhynchoid had small peglike teeth. It had a wingspan of 1 foot (0.3 meters) and probably ate insects. It is one of the few rhamphorhynchoids that had a short tail. It lived during the Late Jurassic Period.

✦ ✦ ✦

1928 (Germany)—Another small rhamphorhynchoid, *Campylognathoides* ("curved jaw form") was described by **Strand**. It had a wingspan of about 3.3 feet (1 meter) and a long tail.

✦ ✦ ✦

1959 (Jordan)—A giant pterosaur was discovered and first named *Titanopteryx* ("titan wing") by French paleontologist **Camille Arambourg**. Known mostly from a neck vertebra, it was one of the largest of all pterosaurs. Because the name *Titanopteryx* had already been used, it was renamed *Arambourgiania* ("for Arambourg") in honor of Arambourg in

1989 by **L. A. Nessov** and **L. J. Borkin**. It was from the Late Cretaceous Period.

✦ ✦ ✦

1964 (China)—Paleontologist **Chung Chien Young** discovered and named *Dsungaripterus* ("Junggar Basin wing"), the first known pterosaur from China. Later discoveries in China and Mongolia revealed this medium-sized pterodactyloid to have a most unusual skull. The tooth-

Dsungaripterus

less tips of its jaws were long and pointed and curved upward. The only teeth it had were flat and in the rear of the mouth. It would appear that it used its jaws to pry up or open shellfish, which it then chewed with its rugged teeth. It was from the Early Cretaceous Period.

✦ ✦ ✦

1969 (Argentina)—A small pterosaur was named *Pterodaustro* ("southern wing") by Argentine paleontologist **José Bonaparte**. This small pterodactyloid was distinguished by extraordinary jaws that made up most of the length of its 9.3-

Pterodaustro

inch- (23.5-centimeter-) long skull. The lower jaw was lined with a comb of long, flexible bristles. Its upper jaw had short, flat teeth. It appears that *Pterodaustro* skimmed the ocean for food, scooping up mouthfuls of water and filtering out tiny creatures, which it would then eat. It lived during the Early Cretaceous Period.

1971 **(Central Asia)**—*Sordes* ("hairy devil") was named by Russian **A. G. Sharov.** This tiny rhamphorhynchoid provided the first indisputable evidence that the bodies of some pterosaurs may have been coated with an insulating layer

Sordes

of fur. Fossil evidence for this long-tailed creature also showed that its leathery wings extended between the hind legs. It lived during the Late Jurassic Period in the area now known as Kazakhstan.

✦ ✦ ✦

1973 **(Italy)**—One of the earliest known pterosaurs was named by **Rocco Zambelli.** Called *Eudimorphodon* ("true two-form tooth"), it dated from the Late Triassic Period. A rhamphorhynchoid with a wingspan of about 3.3 feet (1 meter), it was

Eudimorphodon

probably a good flyer. It had numerous fangs in the front of its jaw, indicating that it was suited for snatching up fish.

✦ ✦ ✦

1975 **(United States)**—The undisputed giant of the pterosaur world was named by **Douglas Lawson** from a fossilized wing discovered in Texas. *Quetzalcoatlus* ("plumed serpent" after the feathered serpent-god worshiped by the Aztecs and Toltecs of ancient Mexico) had a wingspan of 36 to 39 feet (11 to 12 meters). This was substantially larger than the previously accepted pterosaur giant, *Pteranodon.* It lived during the Late Cretaceous Period.

1978 (Italy)—*Peteinosaurus* ("winged lizard") was described from the same Late Triassic rock formation that earlier revealed *Eudimorphodon*, so it, too, ranks as one of the oldest known pterosaurs. It was named by **Rupert Wild**.

✦ ✦ ✦

1983 (China)—The rhamphorhynchoid *Angustinaripterus* ("narrow-nostriled wing") was discovered in a Middle Jurassic Period formation near Zigong. The well-preserved skull with large interlocking pointed teeth in its jaws was similar to specimens of rhamphorhynchoids found in Germany. It was described by **He Xinlu, Yan Daihan**, and **Su Chunkang**.

✦ ✦ ✦

1983 (Brazil)—*Cearadactylus* ("Ceará finger," after a location in Brazil) was described by **Giuseppe Leonardi** and **G. Borgomanero**. This pterodactyloid is known only from a partial skull in which most of the jaw was preserved. It had a set of long, pointed teeth in the snout area and shorter ones in the rear of the mouth. The skull was 22.5 inches (57 centimeters) long. It dates from the Early Cretaceous Period.

✦ ✦ ✦

1985 (Brazil)—One of the best-known pterosaur species from the Early Cretaceous formations of Brazil was named *Anhanguera* ("old devil") by **D. A. Campos** and **Alexander Wilhelm Armin Kellner**. This rhamphorhynchoid had a long snout with widely spaced, short, pointed teeth. It also had a bony crest about halfway down its long snout.

1987 (Brazil)—A rhamphorhynchoid with an unusual crest on the front of its jaw was described by **Peter Wellnhofer**. The top and bottom parts of the jaw had a round, flattened crest. When the mouth was closed, the crests formed a kind of keel like that on a boat. Wellnhofer suggested that the crest helped the pterosaur plow through the water when it was hunting for fish. He

Tropeognathus

named it *Tropeognathus* ("keel jaw"). It lived during the Early Cretaceous Period.

1994 (Brazil)—Eberhard Frey and **David M. Martill** named a new rhamphorhynchoid from the Early Cretaceous deposits of northeastern Brazil. *Arthurdactylus* ("Arthur's finger") was estimated to be about 15 feet (4.5 meters) long. It was named after Sir Arthur Conan Doyle, author of Sherlock Holmes stories and of *The Lost World,* an early science fiction novel in which living pterosaurs were found on an isolated plateau high in the Amazon rain forest.

1995 (United States)—A small pterodactyloid was named *Montanazhdarcho* ("Montana dragon") by **Kevin Padian, Armand de Ricqlès**, and **John Horner**. It lived during the Late Cretaceous Period in what is today Montana.

✦ ✦ ✦

1995 (England)—A pterodactyloid with a flattened snout was named *Plataleorhynchus* ("spoonbill snout") by **S.C.B. Howse**

and **A. R. Milner**. It lived during the Late Jurassic or Early Cretaceous Period.

1997 **(China)**—A new pterodactyloid, *Eosipterus* ("eastern wing"), was named by **Ji Shuan** and **Ji Qiang**. It was probably a filter feeder similar to *Ctenochasma*.

1998 **(France)**—A small pterodactyloid found in the Normandy region of France was named *Normannognathus* ("Normandy jaw") by **Eric Buffetaut, Jean-Jacques Lepage**, and **G. Lepage**. It had a peculiar, triangle-shaped crest on its head. It lived during the Late Jurassic Period.

1999 **(China)**—The only known rhamphorhynchoid pterosaur from the Early Cretaceous Period was named by **Ji Shuan, Ji Qiang**, and **Kevin Padian** as *Dendrorhynchoides* ("tree of *Rhamphorhynchus*"). It was small, with a wingspan of about 16 inches (40 centimeters). This specimen extended the long history of the rhamphorhynchoids into the early part of the Cretaceous Period, whereas previously it had been thought that they all became extinct by the end of the Jurassic Period.

1999 **(North Africa)**—A new pterodactyloid from the Early to Late Cretaceous formations of Morocco was described by **Bryn J. Mader** and **Alexander Wilhelm Armin Kellner**. Called *Siroccopteryx* ("Sirocco wing"), it was similar to

Anhanguera from Brazil. It had a long snout and widely spaced teeth for snatching fish.

2000 (Chile)—*Domeykodactylus* ("Domeyko finger," after Cordillera Domeyko, in the Andes, where the specimen was found) was named by **Eberhard Frey, David M. Martill, G. C. Diaz**, and **C. M. Bell**.

2001 (China)—A large pterosaur from the Early Cretaceous formations of China was named *Haopterus* ("Hao's wing"). It had long and slender teeth and a crestless skull. It is the first indisputable evidence of a pterodactyloid from Asia. It was named by **Wang Xiaolin** and **Lü Junchang**. The two scientists also announced finding evidence of hairlike fibers on the neck of the specimen.

CURRENTLY KNOWN PTEROSAURS

The list below includes the genus names of currently known and scientifically accepted pterosaurs. Each genus name is followed by the name(s) of the paleontologist(s) who described it in print and the year in which it was named.

Angustinaripterus—He, Yan, and Su, 1983

Anhanguera—Campos and Kellner, 1985

Anurognathus—Doederline, 1923

Arambourgiania—Nessov and Borkin, 1989 (previously *Titanopteryx arambourg*, 1959)

Araripedactylus—Wellnhofer, 1977

Araripesaurus—Price, 1971

Arthurdactylus—Frey and Martill, 1994

Azhdarcho—Nessov, 1984

Batrachognathus—Riabinin, 1948

Brasileodactylus—Kellner, 1984

Campylognathoides—Strand, 1928

Cearadactylus—Leonardi and Borgomanero, 1983

Comodactylus—Galton, 1981

Criorhynchus—Owen, 1874

Ctenochasma—von Meyer, 1852

Cycnorhamphus—Seeley, 1870

Dendrorhynchoides—Ji Shuan, Ji Qiang, and Padian, 1999

Dermodactylus—Marsh, 1881

Dimorphodon—Owen, 1859

Diopecephalus—Seeley, 1871

Domeykodactylus—Martill, Frey, Diaz, and Bell, 2000

Doratorhynchus—Seeley, 1875

Dorygnathus—Wagner, 1860

Dsungaripterus—Young, 1964

Eosipterus—Ji Shuan, Ji Qiang, 1997

Eudimorphodon—Zambelli, 1973

Gnathosaurus—von Meyer, 1833

Haopterus—Wang and Lü, 2001

Herbstosaurus—Casamiquela, 1974

Huanhepterus—Dong, 1982

Kepodactylus—Harris and Carpenter, 1996

Mesadactylus—Jensen and Padian, 1989

Montanazhdarcho—Padian, de Ricqlès, and Horner, 1994

Nesodactylus—Colbert, 1969

Noripterus—Young, 1973

Normannognathus—Buffetaut, J.-J. Lepage, and G. Lepage, 1998

Nyctosaurus—Marsh, 1876

Odontorhynchus—Stolley, 1936

Ornithocheirus—Seeley, 1869

Ornithodesmus—Seeley, 1887

Parapsicephalus—Arthaber, 1918

Peteinosaurus—Wild, 1978

Phobetor—Bakhurina, 1986

Plataleorhynchus—Howse and Milner, 1995

Preondactylus—Wild, 1983

Pteranodon—Marsh, 1876

Pterodactylus—Cuvier, 1812

Pterodaustro—Bonaparte, 1969

Puntanipterus—Bonaparte and Sanchez, 1974

Quetzalcoatlus—Lawson, 1975

Rhamphinion—Padian, 1984

Rhamphocephalus—Seeley, 1880

Rhamphorhynchus—von Meyer, 1847

Santanadactylus—de Buisonje, 1980

Scaphognathus—Wagner, 1861

Siroccopteryx—Mader and Kellner, 1999

Sordes—Sharov, 1971

Tapejara—Kellner, 1989

Tropeognathus—Wellnhofer, 1987

Tupuxuara—Kellner and Campos, 1988

Chapter Notes

Chapter 2. The Many Families of Flying Reptiles

1. Paul Sereno, "The Evolution of Dinosaurs," *Science*, June 25, 1999, vol. 284, p. 2137.

2. Based on Peter Wellnhofer, *The Illustrated Encyclopedia of Pterosaurs* (New York: Crescent Books, 1991).

Chapter 3. Anatomy of the Flying Reptiles

1. Peter Wellnhofer, *The Illustrated Encyclopedia of Pterosaurs* (New York: Crescent Books, 1991), p. 153.

2. Wellnhofer, p. 154.

3. Cherrie Bramwell, "The First Hot-Blooded Flappers," *Spektrum*, no. 69, 1970, pp. 12–14.

4. Wellnhofer, p. 46.

5. Philip J. Currie and Kevin Padian, eds., *The Encyclopedia of Dinosaurs* (San Diego: Academic Press, 1997), p. 616.

6. A. G. Sharov, "New Flying Reptiles from the Mesozoic of Kazakhstan and Kirghizia," *Akademia Nauk, Paleontological Institute*, no. 130, 1971, pp. 104–113.

7. David M. Unwin and Natasha N. Bakhurina, "*Sordes pilosus* and the Nature of the Pterosaur Flight Apparatus," *Nature*, no. 371, 1994, pp. 62–64.

8. Wellnhofer, p. 163.

Chapter 4. Lifestyle and Physiology of the Flying Reptiles

1. Tilly Edinger, "Das Gehirn der Pterosaurier," *Zeitschrift für Anatomie und Entwicklungsgeschichte*, vol. 82, no. 1/3, 1927, pp. 105–112.

2. Deborah S. Wharton, "The Evolution of the Avian Brain," *Journal of Vertebrate Paleontology, Abstracts of Papers*, vol. 21, Supplement to no. 3, August 22, 2001, p. 113.

3. Philip J. Currie and Kevin Padian, eds., *The Encyclopedia of Dinosaurs* (San Diego: Academic Press, 1997), p. 616.

4. Peter Wellnhofer, *The Illustrated Encyclopedia of Pterosaurs* (New York: Crescent Books, 1991), p. 163.

5. Harry Govier Seeley, "On the Pterodactyle as Evidence of a New Subclass of Vertebrates (Saurornia)," *Reports of the British Association of Scientists, 34th Meeting*, p. 69.

6. Wellnhofer, p. 157.

7. Carl Steiler, "Neur Rekonstruktionsversuch eines Liassichen Flugsauriers," *Naturwissenschaftliche Wochenschrift*, 1922. vol. 21, no. 20, pp. 273–280.

8. Martin Lockley and Adrian P. Hunt, *Dinosaur Tracks and Other Fossil Footprints of the Western United States* (New York: Columbia University Press, 1995), pp. 158–163.

9. Peter Dodson, "Quantitative Aspects of Relative Growth and Sexual Dimorphism in Protoceratops," *Journal of Paleontology*, vol. 50, pp. 929–940.

10. Peter Wellnhofer, "Die Rhamphorhynchoidea (Pterosauria) der Oberjura-Plattenkalke Süddeutschlands Teil III: Palökologie und Stammersgeschichte." *Palaeontographica* (A), no. 149, 1975, pp. 1–30.

11. Wellnhofer, *The Illustrated Encyclopedia of Pterosaurs*, p. 162.

12. Ibid.

Chapter 5. Eggs and Babies

1. Peter Wellnhofer, *The Illustrated Encyclopedia of Pterosaurs* (New York: Crescent Books, 1991), p. 162.

Chapter 6. Feeding Habits and Adaptations

1. Peter Wellnhofer, *The Illustrated Encyclopedia of Pterosaurs* (New York: Crescent Books, 1991), pp. 159–160.

2. Ibid., p. 159.

3. David M. Unwin, "Variable Growth Rate and Delayed Maturation: Do They Explain Giant Pterosaurs?" *Journal of Vertebrate Paleontology, Abstracts of Papers*, vol. 21, supplement to no. 3, August 22, 2001, pp. 109–110.

GLOSSARY

anatomy—The study of the skeletal and muscular systems of a living organism.

archosaur—A subclass of reptiles that includes crocodilians, dinosaurs (with birds), pterosaurs, and thecodonts.

braincase—The internal portion of the skull that encloses and protects the brain.

convergent evolution—Evolution that occurs when different kinds of animals, although otherwise unrelated, adapt to their environment by developing similar anatomical features. The development of powered flight separately in pterosaurs, birds, and bats is an example of convergent evolution.

Cretaceous Period—The third and final major time division, 144 to 65 million years ago, of the Mesozoic Era. The end of the age of dinosaurs.

ectotherm—Cold-blooded animals whose body temperature is affected by the temperature of their environment and by their behavior. They may actually become warmer than the air temperature while basking in full sunlight. Modern ectotherms include most fish, reptiles, and amphibians.

endotherm—Warm-blooded animals that generate their own body heat internally. They have a constant body temperature no matter what the temperature of their surroundings. Modern endotherms include mammals, birds, and some fish.

evolution—The process of change through time of living organisms.

extinction—The irreversible elimination of an entire species of plant or animal.

femur—The long, large bone of the upper leg.

forewing—A small section of wing that stretches between a pterosaur's wrist and its side.

Jurassic Period—The second of the three major time divisions, 208 to 144 million years ago, of the Mesozoic Era.

Mesozoic Era—The time of the dinosaurs (245 to 65 million years ago).

notarium—Several fused back bones in the upper spine of some pterosaurs that helped anchor the animal's specialized flying structures.

olfactory—Relating to the sense of smell.

optic—Relating to vision.

paleontologist—A scientist who studies life-forms of the geologic past, especially through the analysis of plant and animal fossils.

paleontology—The science of extinct organisms.

pelvis—The hip bones.

physiology—The study of how the biological structures of an organism are used.

predator—A creature that kills other creatures for food.

pterosaur—A flying reptile that lived during the Mesozoic Era.

sexual dimorphism—Differences in size, shape, physiology, and behavior between males and females of the same kind of animal.

trackway—Two or more fossilized footprints of an extinct animal.

Triassic Period—The first of the three major time divisions, 245 to 208 million years ago, of the Mesozoic Era.

vertebra—A bone of the neck, spine, or tail.

vertebrate—Any animal that has a backbone (spine).

FURTHER READING

Brochu, Christopher A., John Long, Colin McHenry, John D. Scanlon, and Paul Willis. *Dinosaurs.* San Francisco: Time-Life Books, 2000.

Currie, Philip J., and Kevin Padian, eds. *Encyclopedia of Dinosaurs.* San Diego: Academic Press, 1997.

Lambert, David. *Dinosaur Encyclopedia: From Dinosaurs to the Dawn of Man.* New York: Dorling Kindersley, 2001.

Norman, David. *The Illustrated Encyclopedia of Dinosaurs.* London: Salamander Books, 1985.

Sternberg, Charles H. *Life of a Fossil Hunter.* New York: Dover, 1990.

Wellnhofer, Peter. *The Illustrated Encyclopedia of Pterosaurs.* New York: Crescent Books, 1991.

Zimmerman, Howard. *Beyond the Dinosaurs!: Sky Dragons, Sea Monsters, Mega-Mammals, and Other Prehistoric Beasts.* New York: Atheneum, 2001.

Internet Addresses

American Museum of Natural History. *Fossil Halls*, n.d. <http://www.amnh.org/exhibitions/Fossil_Halls/index.html>

Creisler, Ben. *Pterosauria Translation and Pronunciation Guide.* ©1996–1999. <http://www.dinosauria.com/dml/names/ptero.htm>

Everhart, Mike. *Sternberg Museum of Natural History.* ©2000–2002. <http://www.oceansofkansas.com/Sternbrg.html>

Scotese, Christopher R. *Paleomap Project.* n.d. <http://www.scotese.com>

The University of California Museum of Paleontology, Berkeley, and the Regents of the University of California. *Introduction to the Pterosauria.* ©1994–2002. <http://www.ucmp.berkeley.edu/diapsids/pterosauria.html>

INDEX

A
airfoils, 35
Angustinaripterus, 30, 88, 91
Anhanguera, 32, 52, 88
Anurognathus, 30, *49*, 72, 85
Arambourg, Camille, 85
Arambourgiania, 33, 85
Araripedactylus, 33
Araripesaurus, 32
Archaeopteryx, *19*, 20, 56, 81
archosaurs, 23, 24, 26
Arthurdactulus, 89
azhdarchids, 77
Azhdarcho, 33

B
Bakhurina, Natasha, 43
Batrachognathus 30
Bell, C. M., 91
Bonaparte, José, 86
Borgomanero, G., 88
Borkin, L. J., 86
braincase, 55
Brasileodactylus, 32
Buckland, William, 19
Buffetaut, Eric, 90

C
Campos, D. A., 88
Campylognathoides, 30, 85
Cearadactylus, 33, 72, 88
Collini, Cosimo Alessandro, 20, 81–82
Comodactylus, 30
convergent evolution, 14, 35
Corythosaurus, *66*
Criorhynchus, 32, 74

Ctenochasma, 31, 73, 83, 90
Cuvier, Georges, 20, 82

D
Dermodactylus, 33
Dendrorhynchoides, 90
Diapsida, 23, 24
Diaz, G. C., 91
Dimorphodon, *30*, 62, 71, *84*
Doederline, 85
Domeykodactylus, 91
Doratorhynchus, 33
Dorygnathus, 30, 42
Dsungaripterus, *32*, 73, 86

E
ectotherms, 59
endotherms, 59
Edinger, Tilly, 55
Eosipterus, 90
Eudimorphodon, *30*, 71, *87*, 88
extinction, 16, 77–79

F
fish, extinct, 71
flight, evolution of, 35–37
Frey, Eberhard, 89, 91

G
Gallodactylus, *31*, 50, 72
geologic time scale, 17
Germanodactylus, 31, *51*, 72
Gnathosaurus, 31, *49*, 50, 73, 82, 83

H
Haopterus, 91
He Xinlu, 88